SECOND EDITION

STEP FORWARD

STANDARDS-BASED LANGUAGE LEARNING
FOR WORK AND ACADEMIC READINESS

SERIES DIRECTOR
Jayme Adelson-Goldstein

Jenni Currie Santamaria

OXFORD
UNIVERSITY PRESS

TABLE OF CONTENTS

Unit	LESSON	LANGUAGE	
	Key Objectives	Vocabulary	Grammar
PRE-UNIT **The First Step** page 2 **Themes** ■ Classroom directions ■ Imperatives	■ Follow classroom directions ■ Use appropriate language to introduce yourself	**Topic-Specific** ■ Classroom directions **OPD Connection** ■ Meeting and Greeting ■ A Classroom	■ Imperatives
1 Please Spell That page 4 **Themes** ■ Introductions ■ Taking messages	■ Identify letters of the alphabet ■ Identify numbers and plural nouns ■ Use nouns and the verb *be* to talk about the classroom ■ Use spelling for clarification ■ Use indefinite articles ■ Interpret a supplies checklist	**Topic-Specific** ■ The alphabet ■ Classroom supplies ■ Numbers ■ Things in a classroom **OPD Connection** ■ Meeting and Greeting ■ Personal Information ■ A Classroom ■ Numbers	■ Singular and plural nouns ■ Subject pronouns and the verb *be* ■ *A/an*
2 How Are You Feeling? page 18 **Themes** ■ Feelings ■ Filling out a form	■ Identify appropriate language to describe feelings and emotions ■ Respond to questions about personal information ■ Describe personal information ■ Use negative statements with *be* to talk about people ■ Respond to personal information questions ■ Express regret ■ Identify the information on an envelope ■ Complete a personal information form	**Topic-Specific** ■ Feeling words ■ Items on a form ■ Parts of an address **OPD Connection** ■ Feelings ■ Personal Information ■ The Post Office	■ *be* + adjective ■ *be from* ■ *in* + place ■ negative statements with *be* in the simple present
3 What Time Is It? page 32 **Themes** ■ Telling time ■ Reading a schedule	■ Interpret time with analog and digital clocks ■ Identify places in the community ■ Describe a work day ■ Use *yes/no* questions and short answers with *be* to talk about time and location ■ Ask for information about places in the community ■ Identify types of transportation ■ Interpret a schedule	**Topic-Specific** ■ Time words and expressions ■ Places in the community ■ Transportation **OPD Connection** ■ Time ■ City Streets ■ Public Transportation **Academic language** *schedule*	■ *It's* + time ■ Prepositions of location and time ■ *Yes/no* questions with *be* and short answers in the simple present

Grammar charts pages 172–176

▶▶ *Step Forward* supports learners as they work to meet the *English Language Proficiency Standards for Adult Education* (ELPS) and the *College and Career Readiness Standards for Adult Education* (CCRS). See *Step Forward's* **Teacher Resource Center** for step-by-step lesson plans that list the level-specific ELP and CCR standards, and for other detailed correlations.

LANGUAGE STRATEGIES		COLLEGE & CAREER READINESS	
Reading & Writing	**Listening & Speaking**	**Critical Thinking**	**Collaboration**
■ Read a conversation	**Conversation** ■ Practice with introductions **Focused Listening** ■ Listen for directions	**Critical thinking** ■ Process instructions	■ Understand teamwork ■ Communicate information ■ Communicate verbally
■ Write about the classroom ■ Read and write phone numbers ■ Read a class supplies list **Writing strategy** ■ Writing a list **Reading strategy** ■ Understanding checkboxes	**Conversation** ■ Listen to and practice a conversation on names and spelling **Focused Listening** ■ Listen for phone numbers ■ Listen for spelling of names ■ Listen for *a/an* **Pronunciation** ■ Practice with *i* and *e* sounds	**Critical thinking** ■ Read, write, and identify numbers ■ Identify phone numbers **Problem solving** ■ Determine how to respond appropriately when you don't understand	■ Communicate information ■ Speak so others can understand ■ Communicate verbally ■ Work with others ■ Understand teamwork
■ Read a registration form ■ Write about personal information ■ Read an envelope ■ Complete a form with personal information **Writing strategy** ■ Writing first and last name on a form	**Conversation** ■ Listen and practice the conversation: "How are you feeling?" **Focused Listening** ■ Listen for personal information **Pronunciation** ■ Practice with number of syllables in words	**Critical thinking** ■ Reflect on feelings ■ Differentiate between first and last names **Problem solving** ■ Determine how to find a correct zip code	■ Listen actively ■ Cooperate with others ■ Communicate information ■ Understand teamwork ■ Work with others ■ Communicate information
■ Write about a typical day ■ Read a work schedule ■ Read a bus schedule **Writing strategy** ■ Writing out time in numbers and words	**Conversation** ■ Ask about times and places ■ Listen and practice the conversation: "Excuse me. What time is it?" **Focused Listening** ■ Listen for times and places ■ Listen for modes of transportation **Pronunciation** ■ Practice with *yes/no* question intonation	**Critical thinking** ■ Interpret clock times ■ Interpret a bus schedule **Problem solving** ■ Identify ways to solve a scheduling conflict	■ Listen actively ■ Communicate information ■ Cooperate with others ■ Communicate verbally

	LESSON	LANGUAGE	
Unit	**Key Objectives**	**Vocabulary**	**Grammar**
4 What Day Is It? page 46 **Themes** ■ Days and months ■ Day and night shifts	■ Identify the days of the week ■ Identify the months of the year ■ Describe an important date ■ Use *on, at, when, where*, and *what time* ■ Use appropriate language to say goodbye ■ Interpret dates on a job application ■ Review questions and answers with *in, on, when, where*, and *what time*	**Topic-Specific** ■ Days of the week ■ Basic calendar words **OPD Connection** ■ The Calendar ■ Time ■ Numbers **Academic language** *registration*	■ *in* + month/year ■ Prepositions of time: *on, at* ■ Information questions: *When, Where, What time* ■ Abbreviations for months and days of the week
5 How Much Is It? page 60 **Themes** ■ Money ■ Calculating sales prices	■ Identify coins and currency ■ Identify common articles of clothing ■ Interpret price tags ■ Describe shopping experiences ■ Use demonstrative pronouns to talk about prices ■ Discuss prices ■ Identify methods of payment ■ Discuss a money problem	**Topic-Specific** ■ Money words ■ Clothing **OPD Connection** ■ Money ■ Everyday Clothes ■ A Classroom ■ Shopping ■ Bathroom **Academic language** *credit card, percent*	■ *How much* questions ■ Demonstratives ■ Singular and plural nouns
6 That's My Son page 74 **Themes** ■ Family members ■ Employee information form	■ Identify friends and family members ■ Describe family members, friends, and marital status ■ Use possessive adjectives and the simple present to discuss family ■ Discuss friends and family members ■ Identify school requirements ■ Interpret a note from a teacher	**Topic-Specific** ■ Families **OPD Connection** ■ Families ■ Schools and Subjects ■ World Map ■ Measurements **Academic language** *emergency contact, marital status*	■ Irregular plurals ■ Possessive adjectives ■ Simple present affirmative statements ■ Information questions

LANGUAGE STRATEGIES		COLLEGE & CAREER READINESS	
Reading & Writing	**Listening & Speaking**	**Critical Thinking**	**Collaboration**
■ Write about your birthday ■ Read a job application **Writing strategy** ■ Using prepositions of time in writing	**Conversation** ■ Listen and practice saying goodbye **Focused Listening** ■ Listen for dates and months ■ Listen for prepositions of time and question words **Pronunciation** ■ Practice with *t* and *th* sounds	**Critical thinking** ■ Interpret a calendar **Problem solving** ■ Determine what to do when late	■ Understand teamwork ■ Communicate information ■ Work with others ■ Communicate verbally ■ Speak so others can understand
■ Write about shopping ■ Read about ways to pay **Writing strategy** ■ Using capital letters **Reading strategy** ■ Interpreting pie charts	**Conversation** ■ Listen and practice a conversation asking about prices in a store **Focused Listening** ■ Listen for money amounts and prices ■ Listen for clothing items ■ Listen for payment methods **Pronunciation** ■ Practice with *s* and *sh* sounds	**Critical thinking** ■ Interpret price tags **Problem solving** ■ Decide what to do when short on cash	■ Use math to solve problems and communicate ■ Understand teamwork ■ Communicate information ■ Work with others ■ Communicate verbally
■ Write about your family and friends ■ Complete an employee information form ■ Read a school note **Writing strategy** ■ Using capital letters and periods in sentences	**Conversation** ■ Introduce with titles and last names ■ Listen and practice a conversation about families and friends **Focused Listening** ■ Listen for titles ■ Listen for family members ■ Listen for heights **Pronunciation** ■ Practice with *who* and *how*	**Critical thinking** ■ Interpret a chart **Problem solving** ■ Decide how a parent should respond to a child who receive a failing grade	■ Use math to solve problems and communicate ■ Understand teamwork ■ Communicate information ■ Cooperate with others ■ Communicate verbally

Table of contents **v**

	LESSON	LANGUAGE	
Unit	**Key Objectives**	**Vocabulary**	**Grammar**
7 Do You Need Apples? page 88 **Themes** ■ Food ■ Supermarket job ads	■ Identify fruit and vegetables ■ Describe food preferences ■ Use the simple present to express likes, dislikes, and needs ■ State needs ■ Identify prices ■ Identify containers ■ Read a shopping list	**Topic-Specific** ■ Fruit and vegetables ■ Food groups ■ Containers **OPD Connection** ■ Fruit ■ Vegetables ■ Meat and Poultry ■ Back from the Market ■ A Grocery Store ■ Containers and Packaging	■ Simple present negative statements ■ Simple present *yes/no* questions and short answers ■ Count and noncount nouns ■ Quantity words with noncount nouns
8 What's the Matter? page 102 **Themes** ■ Health ■ Reporting sickness	■ Identify parts of the body ■ Identify common symptoms and ailments ■ Describe health problems in an email ■ Use *have* and *has* to describe symptoms and ailments ■ Make medical appointments ■ Interpret medical labels	**Topic-Specific** ■ Body parts ■ Health problems **OPD Connection** ■ The Body ■ Symptoms and Injuries ■ Illnesses and Medical Conditions ■ Medical Care ■ Taking Care of Your Health **Academic language** *label, medical*	■ *have* and *has*: simple present statements and *yes/no* questions ■ Frequency expressions
9 What Size? page 116 **Themes** ■ Colors and clothes ■ Dress codes	■ Identify colors and clothes ■ Describe what you are wearing today ■ Use the present continuous to describe clothes ■ Shop for clothes ■ Interpret basic sizes ■ Identify weather conditions	**Topic-Specific** ■ Colors ■ Clothes and sizes ■ Weather conditions **OPD Connection** ■ Colors ■ Seasonal Clothing ■ Everyday Clothes ■ Describing Clothes ■ Weather **Academic language** *dress code*	■ Present continuous affirmative statements ■ Present continuous *yes/no* questions ■ *How much* questions ■ *It's* + weather condition ■ Adjective + noun

LANGUAGE STRATEGIES		COLLEGE & CAREER READINESS	
Reading & Writing	**Listening & Speaking**	**Critical Thinking**	**Collaboration**
■ Write about food preferences ■ Read supermarket job ads ■ Read a shopping list **Writing strategy** ■ Checking written work	**Conversation** ■ Talk about food preferences ■ Listen and practice a conversation asking for help in a store **Focused Listening** ■ Listen for food groups ■ Listen for food prices ■ Listen for food containers **Pronunciation** ■ Practice with final sounds -s and -es	**Critical thinking** ■ Interpret a shopping list ■ Interpret food ads **Problem solving** ■ Determine how to improve poor eating habits	■ Work with others ■ Understand teamwork ■ Communicate information ■ Speak so others can understand ■ Communicate verbally ■ Work with others
■ Read an email ■ Write about health problems ■ Read medicine labels **Writing strategy** ■ Using salutations and closings in notes and emails	**Conversation** ■ Give and follow directions ■ Listen to and practice making a doctor's appointment **Focused Listening** ■ Listen for appointment times ■ Listen for health problems ■ Listen for days and times in a calendar **Pronunciation** ■ Practice with the different sounds of *a*	**Critical thinking** ■ Interpret medicine labels **Problem solving** ■ Determine how to handle obligations when sick	■ Listen actively ■ Understand teamwork ■ Communicate information ■ Work with others ■ Cooperate with others ■ Work with others
■ Write about clothes ■ Read about dress codes ■ Read about weather conditions **Writing strategy** ■ Using commas in a list	**Conversation** ■ Talk about favorite colors ■ Listen to and practice a conversation about shopping for clothes **Focused Listening** ■ Listen for clothes and colors ■ Listen for weather conditions ■ Listen for sizes and prices **Pronunciation** ■ Practice with *I* and *I'm*	**Critical thinking** ■ Interpret a receipt **Problem solving** ■ Decide what to do with an unwanted gift	■ Understand teamwork ■ Cooperate with others ■ Communicate information ■ Work with others ■ Communicate verbally

	LESSON	LANGUAGE	
Unit	**Key Objectives**	**Vocabulary**	**Grammar**
10 **This Is My Home** page 130 **Themes** ■ The home ■ Asking about a rental	■ Identify rooms and things in the home ■ Identify parts of an apartment building ■ Describe your house ■ Use possessive 's ■ Use prepositions to describe a home ■ Ask for information about a home for rent ■ Identify different types of housing ■ Interpret classified ads	**Topic-Specific** ■ Things in the home or apartment ■ Types of housing **OPD Connection** ■ A Bedroom ■ A Kitchen ■ A Living Room ■ A Bathroom ■ Different Places to Live ■ Numbers	■ Possessive 's ■ Prepositions of location
11 **Where's the Bank?** page 144 **Themes** ■ Community ■ Work activities	■ Identify places in the community ■ Describe locations and actions of family and friends ■ Use the present continuous to describe common actions ■ Ask for and give directions ■ Use a city services website	**Topic-Specific** ■ Places in the community ■ Actions **OPD Connection** ■ City Streets ■ Emergencies and Natural Disasters ■ Job Skills **Academic language** *Department of Motor Vehicles (DMV), paragraph*	■ Present continuous verbs ■ Present continuous questions and answers with *What* and *Where*
12 **Yes, I can!** page 158 **Themes** ■ Jobs ■ Job interview skills	■ Identify common occupations ■ Describe jobs and duties ■ Describe job skills ■ Use *can* and *can't* to describe job skills ■ Respond to questions about abilities ■ Interpret a job ad	**Topic-Specific** ■ Jobs ■ Job skills **OPD Connection** ■ Jobs and Occupations ■ Job Skills ■ Job Search **Academic language** *construction worker, dental assistant, dress appropriately, driver's license, use a computer*	■ Simple present actions ■ *Can* and *can't: yes/no* questions

LANGUAGE STRATEGIES		COLLEGE & CAREER READINESS	
Reading & Writing	**Listening & Speaking**	**Critical Thinking**	**Collaboration**
■ Write about a home ■ Read housing ads **Writing strategy** ■ Giving a title to a story	**Conversation** ■ Talk about safety at work and at home ■ Listen to and practice a conversation asking about a home for rent **Focused Listening** ■ Listen for rooms in a home ■ Listen for large numbers ■ Listen for types of housing **Pronunciation** ■ Practice with stressed syllables	**Critical thinking** ■ Interpret classified housing ads **Problem solving** ■ Decide what to do when electric power is out	■ Listen actively ■ Understand teamwork ■ Speak so others can understand ■ Communicate information ■ Work with others ■ Communicate verbally ■ Work with others
■ Write about locations of friends and family ■ Read a city services website **Writing strategy** ■ Identifying a paragraph	**Conversation** ■ Talk about weekly destinations ■ Listen to and practice a conversation about locations **Focused Listening** ■ Listen for places and actions ■ Listen for places in the community **Pronunciation** ■ Practice with *th* sounds	**Critical thinking** ■ Ask for and give directions ■ Distinguish between emergencies and non-emergencies **Problem solving** ■ Decide what to do with noisy neighbors	■ Speak so others can understand ■ Understand teamwork ■ Communicate information ■ Work with others ■ Communicate verbally ■ Listen actively ■ Cooperate with others
■ Write about job skills of friends and family ■ Read about job skills ■ Read job ads	**Conversation** ■ Talk about jobs and job interview skills ■ Practice answering job interview questions **Focused Listening** ■ Listen for job skills ■ Listen for schedules **Pronunciation** ■ Practice with *can* and *can't*	**Critical thinking** ■ Interpret help-wanted ads **Problem solving** ■ Determine how to handle a conflict between social and work obligations	■ Understand teamwork ■ Communicate information ■ Listen actively ■ Work with others ■ Communicate verbally ■ Work with others

WELCOME TO THE SECOND EDITION OF *STEP FORWARD*!

"What's new?" is a question that often greets the arrival of a second edition, but let's start with the similarities between *Step Forward Second Edition* and its predecessor. This edition retains the original's effective instructional practices for teaching adult English language learners, such as focusing on learner outcomes, learner-centered lessons, thematic four-skill integration with associated vocabulary, direct instruction of grammar and pronunciation, focused listening, and sourced texts. It also preserves the instructional flexibility that allows it to be used in classes that meet twice a week, and those that meet every day. Perhaps most significantly, this edition continues to provide the differentiation support for teachers in multilevel settings.

The *College and Career Readiness Standards for Adult Education* (Pimentel, 2013) and the 2016 *English Language Proficiency Standards* echo the research by ACT, Parrish and Johnson, Wrigley, and others linking critical thinking skills, academic language, and language strategies to learners' academic success and employability. Rigorous language instruction is key to accelerating our learners' transition into family-sustaining jobs, civic engagement, and/or post-secondary education. *Step Forward Second Edition* has integrated civic, college, and career readiness skills in every lesson. Each *Step Forward* author considered adult learners' time constraints while crafting lessons that flow from objective to outcome, encouraging and challenging learners with relevant tasks that ensure their growth.

STEP FORWARD KEY CONCEPTS

Our learners' varied proficiency levels, educational backgrounds, goals, and interests make the English language classroom a remarkable place. They also create some instructional challenges. To ensure that your learners leave class having made progress toward their language and life goals, these key concepts underpin the *Step Forward* curriculum.

Effective instruction…

▶ acknowledges and makes use of learners' prior knowledge and critical thinking skills.

▶ helps learners develop the language that allows them to demonstrate their 21st century skills.

▶ contextualizes lessons to support learners' workplace, career, and civic goals.

▶ ensures that each lesson's learning objectives, instructions, and tasks are clear.

▶ differentiates instruction in order to accommodate learners at varying proficiency levels within the same class.

▶ provides informational text (including graphs, charts, and images) that builds and expands learners' knowledge.

STEP FORWARD COMPONENTS

Each level of *Step Forward* correlates to *The Oxford Picture Dictionary*. Each *Step Forward* level includes the following components:

Step Forward Student Book
Twelve thematic units focusing on everyday adult topics, each with six lessons integrating communication, workplace, and academic skills, along with language strategies for accuracy and fluency.

Step Forward Audio Program
The recorded vocabulary, focused listening, conversations, pronunciation, and reading materials from the *Step Forward* Student Book.

Step Forward Workbook
Practice exercises for independent work in the classroom or as homework, as well as "Do the Math" sections.

Step Forward Teacher Resource Center
An online collection of downloadable resources that support the *Step Forward* program. The *Step Forward* Teacher Resource Center contains the following components:

• *Step Forward* Lesson Plans: an instructional planning resource with detailed, step-by-step lesson plans featuring multilevel teaching strategies and teaching tips

• *Step Forward* Multilevel Activities: over 100 communicative practice activities and 72 picture cards; lesson materials that work equally well in single-level or multilevel settings

• *Step Forward* Multilevel Grammar Exercises: multilevel grammar practice for the structures presented in the *Step Forward* Student Book

• *Step Forward* Testing Program: tests for every unit in the *Step Forward* Student Book

• *Step Forward* Literacy Reproducible Activities: literacy activities that correspond to the *Step Forward Introductory Level* Student Book, intended to support pre-beginning or semi-literate level learners

• Correlations: correlations to national standards, including the *College and Career Readiness Standards* and the *English Language Proficiency Standards*

• *Step Forward* Answer Keys and Audio Scripts for the *Step Forward* Student Book and Workbook

Step Forward Classroom Presentation Tool
On-screen *Step Forward* Student Book pages, including audio at point of use and whole-class interactive activities, transform each Student Book into a media-rich classroom presentation tool in order to maximize-heads up learning. The intuitive, book-on-screen design helps teachers navigate easily from page to page.

I know I speak for the authors and the entire *Step Forward* publishing team when I say it's a privilege to serve you and your learners.

Jayme Adelson-Goldstein

Jayme Adelson-Goldstein, Series Director

WELCOME, LEARNERS!

Learning English is a challenge. *Step Forward* can help. Here are some ideas to try.

STUDY THE LISTS, CHARTS, AND NOTES
They give you information about English.

Vocabulary list

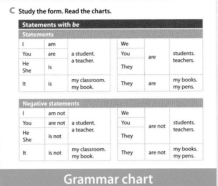

Grammar chart

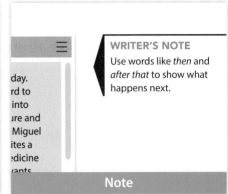

Note

BE BRAVE IN CLASS
Practice helps you use English.

ASK QUESTIONS
Questions help you understand.

COLLABORATE
Work with your classmates, and study alone too.

Work with a partner

Work with a team

Work alone

The First Step

1 Classroom directions

 A Listen and look at the pictures.
1-02

Listen.

Look.

Repeat.

Point.

Write.

Work with a partner.

Read.

Count.

Spell.

 B Listen and check (✓) the picture.
1-03

1. **a**
A-M-Y.
_____

b
1-2-3.
✓

4. **a**
_____

b
_____

2. **a**
_____

b
_____

5. **a**
_____

b
A-M-Y.
_____

3. **a**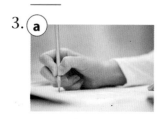
_____

b
_____

6. **a**
_____

b
_____

Follow classroom directions; use appropriate language to introduce yourself

C Listen again. Point and repeat.

1-03

2 Introduce yourself

A Look at the pictures. Read the conversation.

B Listen and read.

1-04

Lorena: Hi, I'm Lorena.

Jin: My name is Jin.

Lorena: Nice to meet you.

Jin: Nice to meet you too.

C Listen again and repeat.

1-04

D Talk to a partner. Make a new conversation. Use your own information.

A: Hi, I'm _____ .

B: My name is _____ .

A: Nice to meet you.

B: Nice to meet you too.

Pre-Unit Lesson 2   **3**

UNIT

1 Please Spell That

A LOOK AT
- Introductions
- Subject pronouns
- Taking messages

LESSON 1 VOCABULARY

1 Learn the alphabet

A Listen and read. Point to the letters in your name.

1-05

The Alphabet

Aa Bb Cc Dd Ee Ff Gg Hh Ii Jj Kk Ll Mm

Nn Oo Pp Qq Rr Ss Tt Uu Vv Ww Xx Yy Zz

B Listen again and repeat.

1-05

C Match the capital letters to the lowercase letters.

a	1. A	e
____	2. B	g
____	3. D	h
____	4. E	q
____	5. G	b
____	6. H	d
____	7. I	a
____	8. Q	i

NEED HELP?

a = ɑ

D Listen. Circle the letter.

1-06

1. (a) i	5. p b
2. i e	6. m n
3. g j	7. y w
4. h j	8. f s

E Work with a partner. Read the letters in 1D.

2 Spell words

 A Look at the pictures. Listen and write the letters you hear.
1-07

1. s _t_ _u_ _d_ _e_ _n_ t

5. p ___ ___ ___ ___ ___ ___

2. t ___ ___ ___ ___ e ___

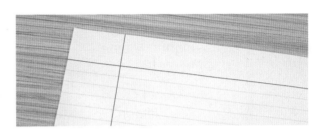

6. p ___ ___ ___ ___

3. b ___ ___ k

7. p ___ ___ ___ ___ ___ ___

4. p ___ ___

8. w ___ ___ ___

B Listen to the words in 2A. Repeat.
1-08

C Copy the words from 2A in your notebook.

▸▸ **TEST YOURSELF**

Work with a partner. Take turns.

Student A: Say a word from 2A.
Student B: Listen and spell the word.

 student

s-t-u-d-e-n-t

ACADEMIC

Unit 1 Lesson 1   **5**

1 Learn numbers 0–19

◆)) **A** Listen and read the numbers.
1-09

0 zero	1 one	2 two	3 three	4 four	5 five	6 six	7 seven

8 eight	9 nine	10 ten	11 eleven	12 twelve	13 thirteen	14 fourteen

15 fifteen	16 sixteen	17 seventeen	18 eighteen	19 nineteen

◆)) **B** Listen again and repeat.
1-09

C Work with a partner. Say the numbers in 1A.

◆)) **D** Look at the pictures. Listen and repeat
1-10 the telephone numbers.

(562) 555-3217   (737) 555-9864

AT WORK ▶ Take messages

◆)) **A** Listen to the phone calls. Write the telephone numbers.
1-11

A-1 Company Phone Calls			
1. Anna Ball	(212) 555 -_____	5. Rita Acoba	(387) 555 -_____
2. Ken Teng	(629) 555 -_____	6. Reem Jarrar	(512) 555 -_____
3. Paula Garcia	(748) 555 -_____	7. Alan Choi	(936) 555 -_____
4. John Nguyen	(256) 555 -_____	8. Uri Kalb	(481) 555 -_____

B Work with a partner. Say a number from A. Point to the numbers.

2 Count things in the classroom

1-12
A Listen and read the numbers.

20 twenty	21 twenty-one	22 twenty-two	23 twenty-three	24 twenty-four	25 twenty-five
26 twenty-six	27 twenty-seven	28 twenty-eight	29 twenty-nine	30 thirty	40 forty
50 fifty	60 sixty	70 seventy	80 eighty	90 ninety	100 one hundred

1-12
B Listen again and repeat.

1-13
C Listen. Write the number of each item.

Classroom A	Classroom B
1. _30_ pencils	6. _____ pencils
2. _____ books	7. _____ books
3. _____ students	8. _____ students
4. _____ pens	9. _____ pens
5. _____ pictures	10. _____ pictures

D Look at 2C. Do the math for Classroom A and Classroom B.

1. How many pencils?   _30 + 22 = 52_
2. How many books?   _____
3. How many students? _____
4. How many pens?   _____
5. How many pictures? _____

E Work with a partner. Say the totals in 2D.

fifty-two pencils

3 Prepare to write: plurals

A Listen and repeat.

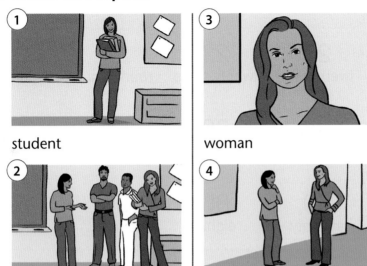

1. student
2. students
3. woman
4. women
5. man
6. men

B Write the new words in your notebook. Practice the words with a partner.

4 Write about your classroom

A Work with a partner. Talk about your classroom.

B Write a list of things in your classroom.

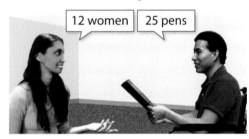

12 women   25 pens

_____

_____

_____

_____

_____

_____

WRITER'S NOTE
Write a List

| 30 pencils |
| 16 women |

▶▶ TEST YOURSELF

Write your phone number.
Next, listen to the teacher.
Write the school phone number.

Your phone number: _____

School phone number: _____

1 Use subject pronouns

A Look at the pictures. Read the words.

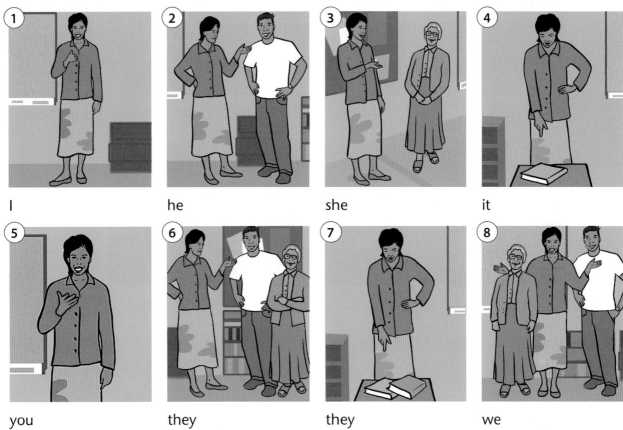

1	2	3	4
I	he	she	it

5	6	7	8
you	they	they	we

B Look at the words in 1A. Listen and repeat.

1-15

C Look at the pictures. Circle *a* or *b*.

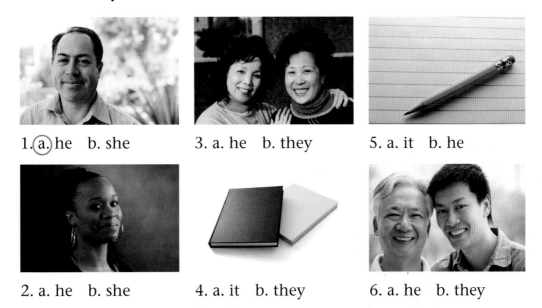

1. a. he   b. she   3. a. he   b. they   5. a. it   b. he

2. a. he   b. she   4. a. it   b. they   6. a. he   b. they

2 Use the verb *be*

1-16
A Look at the pictures. Listen and repeat the sentences.

I <u>am</u> a student.

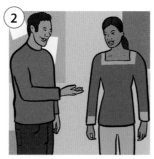
<u>She is</u> a student.

<u>He is</u> a student.

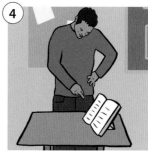
<u>It is</u> a book.

<u>They are</u> students.

<u>We are</u> students.

<u>You are</u> a student.

B Match the parts of the sentence.

_d_	1. I	a. is a teacher.
____	2. They	b. are students.
____	3. It	c. are a student.
____	4. She	d. am a student.
____	5. You	e. is a pencil.

C Complete the sentences. Use *am*, *is*, or *are*.

1. I __am__ a student.
2. You _____ a student.
3. They _____ teachers.
4. He _____ a teacher.
5. It _____ a pen.
6. She _____ Anna.
7. We _____ students.
8. They _____ books.

D Work with a partner. Talk about your classroom. Use *He is*, *She is*, *They are*, or *It is*.

A: She is a student. He is a man.

B: It is a pencil. They are pens.

3 Talk about things and people in a classroom

1-17 **A** Look at the pictures. Listen and repeat the words.

1 clock	2 clocks	3 student	4 students
5 desk	6 desks	7 table	8 tables
9 chair	10 chairs	11 Celia	12 Ron

1-18 **B** Listen and repeat the sentences.

1. It is a clock.
2. They are clocks.
3. She is Celia.
4. They are students.

C Work with a partner. Talk about the pictures in 3A. Use *He, She, It,* and *They*.

It is a clock.
They are clocks.
She is Celia.

D Write sentences about three of the pictures in 3A.

> **NEED HELP?**
>
> **Making a sentence**
> **I**t is a clock**.**
> **H**e is a teacher**.**
> **I**t is a table. **H**e is a student.
> **T**hey are chairs**.**

▸▸ **TEST YOURSELF**

Work with a partner. Look at the pictures in 1A. Make four sentences.

1 Listen for spelling

A Listen. Circle *a* or *b*.
1-19

1. a. Mary   b. Mark   4. a. Sandy   b. Sandi
2. a. John   b. Joan   5. a. Gerry   b. Jerry
3. a. Mel   b. Mal   6. a. Corbin   b. Corvin

B Listen again and check your answers.
1-19

C Listen. Write the names on the nametags.
1-20

HELLO
MY NAME IS

Gina

2 Practice your pronunciation

A Listen for *i* and *e* sounds.
1-21

i	e
1. nice	5. meet
2. write	6. read
3. five	7. repeat
4. sign	8. please

B Listen and check (✓) the sounds you hear.
1-22

	i	e
1.		
2.		
3.		
4.		

C Listen again and repeat.
1-22

3 Make conversation: ask for spelling

A Look at the pictures. Read the conversation.

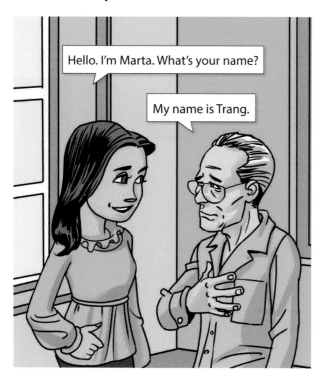

B Listen and read.

1-23

Marta: Hello. I'm Marta. What's your name?

Trang: My name is Trang.

Marta: Please spell that.

Trang: T-R-A-N-G. Trang

C Listen again and repeat.

1-23

D Talk to a partner. Make a new conversation. Use your own information.

A: Hello. I'm _____ . What's your name?

B: My name is _____ .

A: How do you spell that?

B: _____ .

▶▶ TEST YOURSELF

Talk to three classmates. Write their names in the chart. Ask, "Please spell that."

1.	
2.	
3.	

1 Get ready to read

A Notice *a* and *an*. Look at the pictures. Listen and repeat.

1-24

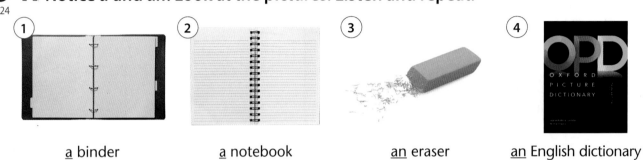

①	②	③	④
<u>a</u> binder	<u>a</u> notebook	<u>an</u> eraser	<u>an</u> English dictionary

B Listen. Write *a* or *an*.

1-25

1. __a__ notebook
2. _____ eraser
3. _____ binder
4. _____ English dictionary

5. _____ pen
6. _____ chair
7. _____ English class
8. _____ teacher

C Look at the pictures. Read the words.

① adult school

③ supplies

② bring

④ pages

D Check (✓) the supplies you bring to school.

- ☐ a pencil
- ☐ a pen
- ☐ an eraser
- ☐ a binder
- ☐ an English dictionary

2 Read a class supplies list

A Read the list.

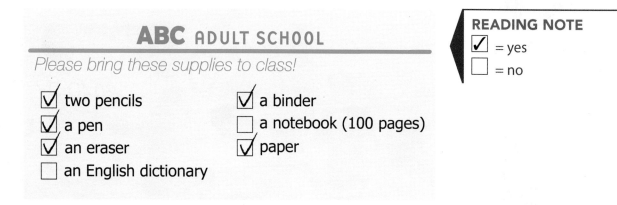

ABC ADULT SCHOOL

Please bring these supplies to class!

☑ two pencils   ☑ a binder
☑ a pen   ☐ a notebook (100 pages)
☑ an eraser   ☑ paper
☐ an English dictionary

READING NOTE
☑ = yes
☐ = no

B Look at the list. Circle *yes* or *no*.

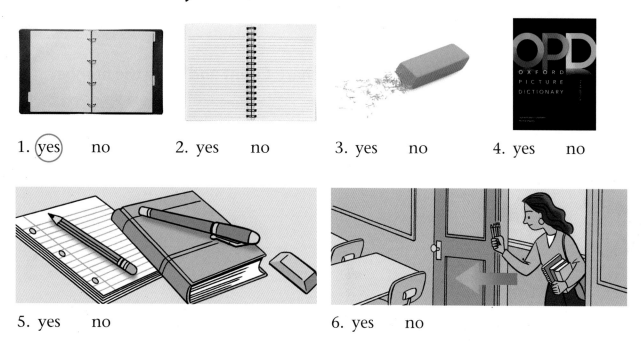

1. (yes)   no   2. yes   no   3. yes   no   4. yes   no

5. yes   no   6. yes   no

 BRING IT TO LIFE

Make a list of supplies for English class.

Bring the list and the supplies to class.

TEAMWORK & LANGUAGE REVIEW

A Work with a team. Talk about the picture. Say what you see.

B Write the words you know in the chart. Count and write the number.

Number	Word
3	men

C Look up three words you don't know in a dictionary.
Add them to the chart.

D Write the words in your notebook. Use alphabetical (A-B-C) order.

book

chair

clock

E Count the things in the picture. Complete the sentences.

1. __It__ is a clock.
2. _____ are books.
3. It _____ a chair.
4. It is _____ pencil.
5. They _____ students.
6. She _____ a woman.

F Write two more sentences about the pictures.

1. _____

2. _____

PROBLEM SOLVING AT WORK

1-26

A Listen. Look at the pictures.

Joel's Problem

a. Say, "Excuse me?"

B Work with your classmates. Help Joel.

a. Say, "Excuse me."

b. Say, "I'm sorry. I don't understand."

LESSON **1** VOCABULARY

1 Learn feeling words

A Look at the pictures. Say what you see.

🔊 **B** Listen and point to the pictures.
1-27

🔊 **C** Listen and repeat the words.
1-27

1. fine	2. happy	3. excited	4. sad
5. hungry	6. thirsty	7. tired	8. sick

D Say the new words with a partner.

E Work with a partner. Cover the words. Point to the pictures. Say the words.

2 Talk about feelings

A Look at the picture. Complete the words.

1. e x __c__ i t e d
2. s ___ d
3. ___ i n e
4. t i r ___ d
5. h a p ___ y
6. t h i r s ___ y
7. ___ u n g r y
8. ___ i c k

B Copy the words from 2A in your notebook.

C Listen and repeat.

1-28

Zita   Inez

Al   Lam

1. **Zita:** I'm tired.
   Inez: I'm tired too.

2. **Al:** I'm hungry.
   Lam: I'm thirsty.

D Talk to a partner. Practice the conversations. Use your own ideas.

1. **A:** I'm _____ .
   B: I'm _____ too.

2. **A:** I'm _____ .
   B: I'm _____ .

▶▶ TEST YOURSELF

Use your notebook. Copy the chart.
Put words from the lesson in the chart.

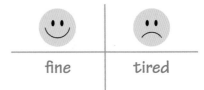

fine | tired

1 Learn about countries

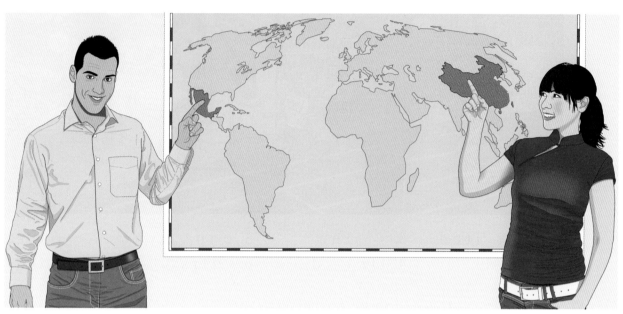

A Listen to the conversation. Point to Marco and Jia.

1-29

B Complete the sentences.

1. Marco is from _____ .

2. Jia is from _____ .

3. I'm from _____ .

C Talk to three partners. Point to your country on a map.

A: Where are you from?

B: I'm from _____ .

D Look at the graph. Complete the sentences.

1. __21__ students are from Mexico.

2. _____ students are from Russia.

3. _____ students are from Cuba.

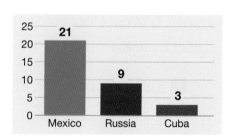

E Work with your classmates. Make a graph like the one in 1D. Then write sentences about your class.

_____ students are from _____ .

ACADEMIC

2 Prepare to write: personal information

A Look at the form. Point to the country.

B Listen and repeat the words.

1-30

1. city
2. state
3. birthplace
4. country

C Listen and read Camille's story.

1-31

1. My first name is Camille.
2. My last name is Preval.
3. I'm from Haiti.
4. Now I live in Dallas, Texas.
5. I'm happy in Dallas.

D Complete the sentences with the words from 2B.

1. Texas is a ____state____ .
2. Dallas is a _____ .
3. Haiti is a _____ .
4. The United States is a _____ too.
5. Dallas is not Camile's _____ .

Camille

E Listen and check your answers from 2D.

1-32

F Listen to Sameen's story. Circle the correct word.

1. My _____ is Sameen.
   a. first name   b. last name

2. My _____ is Hosseini.
   a. first name   b. last name

3. I'm _____ Iran.
   a. in   b. from

4. Now I live _____ Chicago, Illinois.
   a. in   b. from

G Listen again and check your answers.

3 Write about personal information

A Complete the sentences. Use your own information.

My name is _____ .

I'm from _____ .

Now I live in _____ .

B Read your sentences to a partner.

AT WORK ▸ Filling out a form

EMPLOYEE INFORMATION

City: _____, State: _____

Name: _____
          last   first

Birthplace: _____

WRITER'S NOTE

Garcia, Maria
  Last   First

My name is Maria Garcia.

▸▸ **TEST YOURSELF**

Talk to a partner. Copy the sentences. Then complete the sentences.
Use your information and your partner's information.

I'm from _____ . _____ is from _____ . Now we live in _____ .

1 Use negative statements with *be*

A Look at the pictures. Read the sentences.

He is not sick. He is hungry.

She is not sick. She is tired.

B Underline the negative sentences in 1A.

C Study the form. Read the chart. Listen and repeat.

1-34

The Simple Present with *Be*		
Negative Statements		
I	am	
You	are	
He She It	is	not tired.
We They	are	

D Complete the sentences. Use *am not*, *is not*, or *are not*.

He is happy.

1. He _____ sad.
2. He _____ excited.

She is sick.

3. She _____ fine.
4. She _____ happy.

They are tired.

5. They _____ excited.
6. They _____ happy.

2 Use contractions with *be*

A Look at the pictures. Listen and read the sentences.

He's from Mexico.
He's not from Texas.
He isn't from Arizona.

It's a state.
It's not a city.
It isn't a country.

They're in Colorado.
They're not in Texas.
They aren't in New York.

B Underline the negative sentences in 2A.

C Study the grammar. Read the chart. Listen and repeat.

1-36

Be	
Contractions	**Negative contractions**
I am = I'm you are = you're he is = he's she is = she's it is = it's we are = we're they are = they're	I'm not you're not = you aren't he's not = he isn't she's not = she isn't it's not = it isn't we're not = we aren't they're not = they aren't

D Match the sentences.

___c___ 1. I am not tired.

_____ 2. She is not tired.

_____ 3. She is tired.

_____ 4. It is not a state.

_____ 5. They are happy.

_____ 6. They are not happy.

_____ 7. You are not thirsty.

a. You're not thirsty.

b. They're happy.

c. I'm not tired.

d. They're not happy.

e. She's not tired.

f. It's not a state.

g. She's tired.

E Complete the sentences. Use contractions.

1. She 's_____ excited.   2. He _____ sick.   3. They _____ sad.
   She _____ tired.   He _____ happy.   They _____ happy.

3 Talk about feelings

A Look at the picture. Point to Ana. Listen and repeat.

A: Ana isn't happy.

B: She's sad.

B Work with a partner. Talk about the picture in 3A. Use *he*, *she*, *it*, and *they*.

It's the United States.

It isn't Canada.

He's hungry.

C Write three sentences about the picture in 3A.

She's sad. She isn't sad. He's thirsty.

▶▶ TEST YOURSELF

Look the pictures on page 19, 2C. Write two sentences about Zita and two sentences about Lam.

Zita: _____She's tired._____   Lam: _____

_____   _____

1 Listen for personal information questions

A Match the questions to the answers.

_____ 1. How are you today?   a. My name is Ann.
_____ 2. What's your name?   b. I'm from Brazil.
_____ 3. Where are you from?   c. I'm tired.

B Listen. Circle *a* or *b*.

1-38

1. a. How are you today?   b. Where are you from?
2. a. Where are you from?   b. What's your name?
3. a. How are you today?   b. What's your name?

C Listen and choose the answer. Circle *a* or *b*.

1-39

1. a. I'm happy.   b. My name is Pao.
2. a. I'm from China.   b. My name is Leila.
3. a. I'm tired.   b. I'm from China.
4. a. My name is Luis.   b. I'm from Mexico.

2 Practice your pronunciation

A Listen and count the syllables (•).

1-40

1 syllable	2 syllables		3 syllables		
fine	hap	py	ex	cit	ed
•	•	•	•	•	•

B Listen and check (✓) the correct boxes.

1-41

	1. fine	2. thirsty	3. telephone	4. hungry	5. sad	6. twenty-three
1 syllable	✔					
2 syllables						
3 syllables						

C Listen again and check your answers. Then repeat the words.

1-41

3 Make conversation: ask about feelings

A Look at the pictures. Read the conversation.

B Listen and read.

Pedro: How are you feeling?

Vanna: I'm fine. How are you?

Pedro: I'm sick.

Vanna: Oh, I'm sorry.

C Listen again and repeat.

D Talk to a partner. Make a new conversation. Use your own ideas.

A: How are you feeling?

B: I'm _____ . How are you?

A: I'm _____ .

B: Oh, _____ .

NEED HELP?

I'm happy.   I'm sad.

I'm excited.   I'm tired.

▶▶ TEST YOURSELF

Ask and answer the question with three classmates:

How are you feeling?

1 Get ready to read

A Look at the picture. Listen and repeat.

1-43

1. address
2. zip code

B Match.

_____ 1. address   a. 92110

_____ 2. state   b. California

_____ 3. zip code   c. 2091 Oak Street, San Diego, California 92110

_____ 4. city   d. San Diego

C Look at the pictures. Read the words.

NEED HELP?
GA = Georgia
NC = North Carolina

READING NOTE
St. = Street

1. envelope
2. return address
3. mailing address
4. form
5. email

D Complete a form. Use your own information.

EMPLOYEE INFORMATION

_____

number   street

_____

city   state   zip code

2 Read a form and an envelope

A Read the form and the envelope.

River City Adult School
Student Information

Susan   Kirkwood
first name   last name

609   First Street
number   street

Atlanta,   GA   74354
city   state   zip code

SusanKirkwood@email.com
email

Susan Kirkwood
609 First Street
Atlanta, GA 74354

River City Adult School
3712 Maple Street
Salem, NC 60611

B Look at the form and the envelope. Circle *a* or *b*.

1. Susan is in _____ .
   a. Atlanta   b. Salem

2. River City Adult School is in _____ .
   a. Atlanta   b. Salem

3. The address of the school is _____ .
   a. 609 First Street   b. 3712 Maple Street

4. Susan's zip code is _____ .
   a. 609   b. 74354

5. Susan's email is _____ .
   a. SusanKirkwood@email.com   b. Atlanta

 BRING IT TO LIFE

Bring an envelope to class. Circle the mailing address.

Check (✔) the return address.

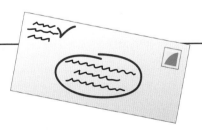

A Work with a team. Talk about the picture. Say what you see.

B Write the words you know in the chart.

Things	Feelings	Other

C Look up three words you don't know in a dictionary. Add them to the chart.

D Look at the numbers in the picture. Complete the sentences. Use contractions.

1. _____They're_____ women. _____ men.
2. _____ thirsty. _____ sick.
3. _____ excited. _____ tired.
4. _____ a country. _____ a city.

E Write two more sentences about the picture.

1. _____
2. _____

PROBLEM SOLVING

A Listen. Look at the pictures.

1-44

Gary's Problem

B Work with your classmates. Help Gary.

 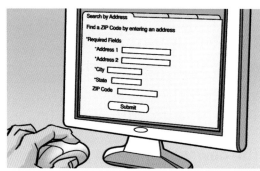

a. Go to the post office. Ask for help.   b. Look on the computer.

UNIT

3 What Time Is It?

A LOOK AT
- Telling time
- *Yes/No* questions with *be*
- Reading a schedule

LESSON 1 VOCABULARY

1 Learn to tell time

A Look at the picture. Count the clocks.

B Listen and point to the pictures.
1-45

C Listen and repeat the words.
1-45

1. morning
2. afternoon
3. evening
4. night
5. 2:00

6. 2:15
7. 2:30
8. 2:45
9. noon
10. midnight

NEED HELP?

2:00 = two o'clock
2:15 = two fifteen
2:30 = two thirty
2:45 = two forty-five

D Say the new words with a partner.

E Work with a partner. Cover the words. Point to the pictures. Say the words.

2 Talk about time

A Look at the pictures. Complete the words.

1. m __o__ r n i n g
2. n ____ o n
3. a ____ t e r n o o n
4. e ____ e n i n g
5. n i g ____ t
6. m i d n ____ g h t

B Copy the words from 2A in your notebook.

C Listen and repeat.

1-46

A: What time is it?

B: It's 6:30.

D Talk to a partner. Point to the clocks in 1B and 2A. Practice the conversation.

A: What time is it?

B: It's _____ .

▶▶ TEST YOURSELF

Work with a partner. Look at the pictures in 1B and 2A. Say a sentence. Take turns.

It's morning.

It's 2:00.

1 Learn about times and places

A Look at the pictures. Read the times and sentences.

8 a.m. = 8:00 in the morning   8 p.m. = 8:00 in the evening

B Listen. Circle *morning* or *evening*.
1-47

1. morning   evening   3. morning   evening
2. morning   evening   4. morning   evening

C Listen again. Write the times you hear.
1-47

1. ___7 a.m.___   2. _____   3. _____   4. _____

D Look at the pictures. Listen for the places.
1-48

1. park   8 a.m.

3. clinic   3 p.m.

2. post office   11 a.m.

4. laundromat   8 p.m.

E Work with a partner. Point to the pictures in 2D. Talk about the pictures.

A: He's at the park.

B: It's 8:00.

A: He's at the _____ .

B: It's _____ .

2 Prepare to write: my day

A Look at the pictures. Say the times.

①

8:00

②

3:30

③

5:00

④

7:00

⑤

9:00

B Listen and repeat the words.

1-49

1. work
2. school
3. the library
4. the store
5. home

C Listen and read Cindy's story.

1-50

1. I go to work at 8 a.m.
2. I go to school at 3:30 p.m.
3. I go to the library in the afternoon.
4. I go to the store in the evening.
5. Now it's 9 p.m. I'm at home.

> **WRITER'S NOTE**
> eight o'clock =
> 8:00 or 8 p.m. / 8 a.m.

D Listen to Rick's story. Circle the correct word.

1. I go to _____ at noon.

   a. the store   b. school

2. I go to _____ in the afternoon.

   a. the park   b. the post office

3. Now it's 4 p.m. I'm at _____ .

   a. the laundromat   b. the library

4. I go to _____ at 6 p.m.

   a. the park   b. work

Rick

E Listen again and check your answers.

3 Write about your day

A Write about your day. Complete the sentences. Use your own ideas.

I go to school at _____ .

I go home at _____ .

Now it's _____ . I'm at _____ .

B Read your story to a partner.

AT WORK   ▶ **Read a schedule**

A Read the work schedule. Who works in the morning?

B Look at the schedule. Circle yes or no.

Work Schedule		
Chris		2 p.m.–5:30 p.m.
Ria	8 a.m.–11 a.m.	12 p.m.–4 p.m.
Diana	7 a.m.–12 p.m.	

1. Chris works in the morning.   Yes   No

2. Diana works in the afternoon.   Yes   No

3. Chris, Ria, and Diana work in the evening.   Yes   No

4. Ria works in the morning and afternoon.   Yes   No

▶▶ TEST YOURSELF

Answer the questions. Write sentences:

Where are you? _____

What time is it? _____

1 Learn about *yes/no* questions with *be*

A Look at the pictures. Read the questions.

Are you at school?

Is it 6:00?

Is he at the library?

🔊
1-52

B Study the form. Read the chart. Listen and repeat.

The Simple Present with *Be*		
yes/no **Questions**		
Is	he she	at school?
	it	6:00?
Are	you they	at home?

C Complete the questions. Use *Is* or *Are*.

1. __Is__ she at school?

2. _____ he at school?

3. _____ it 6:00?

4. _____ they at home?

5. _____ they at home?

6. _____ she at the laundromat?

D Ask and answer the questions in 1C with a partner.

A: Is she at school?

B: Yes.

Use *yes/no* questions and short answers with *be* to talk about time and location   **37**

E Complete the statements and questions. Use *?* or *.*

1. She's at school ___.___   5. He's at the library _____
2. Is she at school _____   6. She's at home _____
3. Is it 5:00 _____   7. Is he at the park _____
4. It's 2:30 _____   8. Are they at the store _____

2 Use short answers with *be*

A Listen. Repeat the questions and answers.

1-53

Al: Are you at the store?

Nell: <u>Yes, I am</u>.

Nell: Are you at work?

Al: <u>No, I'm not</u>.

B Talk to a partner. Ask the questions. Answer with *Yes, I am.* or *No, I'm not.*

1. Are you at school?
2. Are you at the library?
3. Are you a student?
4. Are you tired?
5. Are you at home?
6. Are you happy?
7. Are you from Mexico?
8. Are you from China?
9. Are you at the park?
10. Are you at the laundromat?

C Talk to your classmates about you and your partner.

He's from Mexico.   *She's tired.*   *We are at school.*

3 Ask and answer questions with *be*

 A Listen. Repeat the questions and answers.

1-54

1.
A: Is she at work?
B: Yes, she is.
A: Is she at the clinic?
B: No, she's not.

2.
A: Is he at school?
B: Yes, he is.
A: Is he at the library?
B: No, he's not.

3.
A: Are they at the library?
B: Yes, they are.
A: Are they at home?
B: No, they're not.

B Look at the pictures. Write the answers.

GRAMMAR NOTE
No, he's not. = No, he isn't.
No, she's not. = No, she isn't.
No, it's not. = No, it isn't.
No, they're not. = No, they aren't.

1. Is he at the store?
   Yes, _____ .

2. Is he at the park?
   No, _____ .

3. Is she at home?
   No, _____ .

4. Is she at the clinic?
   Yes, _____ .

C Work with a partner. Point to the pictures in 3A and 3B. Ask and answer new questions.

Is she at the store? No, she's not.

Is she at work? Yes, she is.

▶▶ TEST YOURSELF

Work with a partner. Look at the pictures on pages 34 and 35. Ask and answer the questions. Use short answers.

Take turns.

1 Listen for times

A Listen and point to the pictures.

1-55

B Listen again. What times do you hear? Circle *a* or *b*.

1-55

1. a. 10 a.m.   b. 10 p.m.

2. a. 8:00 in the morning   b. 8:00 in the evening

3. a. 9:00 a.m.   b. 9:00 p.m.

4. a. 10:00 in the morning   b. 10:00 at night

2 Practice your pronunciation

A Listen to the questions.

1-56

1. Is the store open?

2. Are you at the post office?

B Listen and repeat the questions.

1-57

1. Is it 4:00?

2. Is Daniel at the store?

3. Is the class in the morning?

4. Are you at home?

5. Are they happy?

6. Is he at the clinic?

7. Are they at work?

8. Are you hungry?

C Work with a partner. Read the questions in 2B.

3 Make conversation: ask about time

A Look at the pictures. Read the conversation.

B Listen and read.

Alfredo: Excuse me. What time is it?

Pilar: It's 8:00.

Alfredo: Is the store open?

Pilar: No, it's not.

1-58

C Listen again and repeat.

1-58

D Talk to a partner. Practice the conversation. Use your own ideas.

A: Excuse me. What time is it?

B: It's _____ .

A: Is the _____ open?

B: No, it's not.

NEED HELP?

clinic?
library?
school?

Yes, it is.
No, it's not.
Sorry, I don't know.

▸▸ **TEST YOURSELF**

Ask and answer the question with three classmates.

Excuse me. What time is it?   Is the _____ open?

1 Get ready to read

1-59

A Look at the pictures. Listen and repeat the words.

1. bus　　　　2. car　　　　3. plane　　　　4. train

1-60

B Listen to the sentences. Circle *a* or *b*.

1. a. 　　b. 　　　　3. a. 　　b.

2. a. 　　b. 　　　　4. a. 　　b.

C Look at the pictures. Read the words.

hour　　　　　　　minute　　　　　　　12 hours

A: How long is the trip to Newport?

B: It's one hour and 30 minutes.

D Work with your classmates. How long is your trip to school? How long is your English class?

2 Read a bus schedule

A Read the bus schedule.

Bus #	Newport	Springfield	Salem	Sundale
23	7:00 a.m.	—	10:00 a.m.	10:30 a.m.
61	7:30 a.m.	9:00 a.m.	10:50 a.m.	11:20 a.m.
94	9:30 a.m.	11:00 a.m.	—	1:10 p.m.
57	4:00 p.m.	—	7:00 p.m.	7:30 p.m.

> **READING NOTE**
> # = number

B Look at the schedule. Circle the time.

1. Bus 94 is in Springfield. What time is it?   10:00 a.m.   11:00 a.m.
2. Bus 61 is in Newport. What time is it?   7:00 a.m.   7:30 a.m.
3. Bus 23 is in Sundale. What time is it?   10:00 a.m.   10:30 a.m.
4. Bus 57 is in Salem. What time is it?   7:00 a.m.   7:00 p.m.

C Look at the schedule. Answer the questions for Carlos. Circle *a* or *b*.

1. How long is the trip to Sundale on Bus 23?
   a. 2 hours and 30 minutes
   b. 3 hours and 30 minutes
2. How long is the trip to Sundale on Bus 61?
   a. 3 hours and 30 minutes
   b. 3 hours and 50 minutes
3. How long is the trip to Sundale on Bus 94?
   a. 2 hours and 40 minutes
   b. 3 hours and 40 minutes
4. What time is the last bus?
   a. 4:00 p.m.
   b. 7:00 p.m.

Carlos is in Newport.

 BRING IT TO LIFE

Find a bus or a train schedule on your phone or on a computer.

Copy one new word in your notebook.

A Work with a team. Talk about the picture. Say what you see.

B Write the words you know in the chart.

Places	Things	Other

C Look up three words you don't know in a dictionary. Add them to the chart.

D Use your notebook. Write the words from your chart in alphabetical order.

bus

car

clock

E Look at the picture. Complete the questions and answers.

1. **A:** Is Song at the library?

   B: No, _she's not or she isn't_ .

2. **A:** Is Natal at the school?

   B: Yes, _____ .

3. **A:** Is it 4:00?

   B: No, _____ .

4. **A:** Are the students at the school?

   B: Yes, _____ .

5. _____ a teacher?

   Yes, he is.

6. _____ students?

   Yes, they are.

7. _____ Taj at home?

   No, he isn't.

8. _____ Natal at the park?

   No, he isn't.

F Write a new question and answer about the picture.

1. _____ ?

2. _____

PROBLEM SOLVING

A Listen. Look at the pictures.

1-61

Tony's Problem

B Work with your classmates. Help Tony.

a. Leave class early.

b. Go to class late.

UNIT

4 What Day Is It?

A LOOK AT
- Days and months
- *On* and *at*
- Day and night shifts

LESSON 1 VOCABULARY

1 Learn the days of the week

A Look at the calendar. What time is English class?

🔊 **B** Listen and point to the days.
1-62

Sunday	Monday	Tuesday	Wednesday	Thursday	Friday	Saturday
①1	②2	③3	④4	⑤5	⑥6	⑦7
		9:00 – 12:00 English class	3:00 clinic			
	1	2	3	4	5	6

⑧

⑨

Today is Thursday.
Tomorrow is Friday.

THURSDAY 4 ⑩

FRIDAY 5 ⑪

SATURDAY 6

SUNDAY 7 ⑫

🔊 **C** Listen and repeat the words.
1-62

1. Sunday   5. Thursday   9. week
2. Monday   6. Friday   10. today
3. Tuesday   7. Saturday   11. tomorrow
4. Wednesday   8. day   12. weekend

D Say the new words with a partner.

E Work with a partner. Cover the words in 1C. Point to the calendar in 1B.
Say the words.

2 Talk about the days of the week

A Look at the pictures. Complete the words.

1. w e e __k__ e n d
2. M ____ n d a y
3. T u e s ____ a y

4. ____ e d n e s d a y
5. T h ____ r s d a y
6. F r i d a ____

7. S a t u ____ d a y
8. S u n d ____ y
9. w e ____ k

B Copy the words from 2A in your notebook.

C Listen and repeat.

1-63

A: What day is it?

B: It's Thursday.

D Talk to a partner. Point to the calendar. Practice the conversation.

S	M	T	W	Th	F	S

A: What day is it?

B: It's _____ .

▶▶ TEST YOURSELF

Work with a partner. Point to the calendar in 2D. Say a sentence. Take turns.

A: Today is Tuesday.

B: Tomorrow is Wednesday.

A: Today is Thursday.

B: Tomorrow is Friday.

1 Learn about the months

A Look at the picture. Point to the number 24.

B Listen and repeat the months.

1. January	5. May	9. September
2. February	6. June	10. October
3. March	7. July	11. November
4. April	8. August	12. December

C Read the abbreviation. Write the month.

1. Jan. _January_	5. May _____	9. Sep. _____
2. Feb. _____	6. Jun. _____	10. Oct. _____
3. Mar. _____	7. Jul. _____	11. Nov. _____
4. Apr. _____	8. Aug. _____	12. Dec. _____

2 Prepare to write: ordinal numbers

A Look at the calendar. Listen and point to the dates.

Sun.	Mon.	Tues.	Wed.	Thurs.	Fri.	Sat.
1 first	**2** second	**3** third	**4** fourth	**5** fifth	**6** sixth	**7** seventh
8 eighth	**9** ninth	**10** tenth	**11** eleventh	**12** twelfth	**13** thirteenth	**14** fourteenth
15 fifteenth	**16** sixteenth	**17** seventeenth	**18** eighteenth	**19** nineteenth	**20** twentieth	**21** twenty-first
22 twenty-second	**23** twenty-third	**24** twenty-fourth	**25** twenty-fifth	**26** twenty-sixth	**27** twenty-seventh	**28** twenty-eighth
29 twenty-ninth	**30** thirtieth	**31** thirty-first				

March

B Match the ordinal numbers.

_c_ 1. 1st   a. second   ____ 6. 21st   a. twenty-third

____ 2. 2nd   b. fourth   ____ 7. 22nd   b. twenty-fifth

____ 3. 3rd   c. first   ____ 8. 23rd   c. twenty-first

____ 4. 4th   d. fifth   ____ 9. 24th   d. twenty-second

____ 5. 5th   e. third   ____ 10. 25th   e. twenty-fourth

C Listen and write the ordinal number.

1. March _____   5. August _____

2. July _____   6. December _____

3. April _____   7. June _____

4. February _____   8. January _____

D Listen again and repeat the dates in 2C.

E Listen and read Olga's story.

1. It's October.

2. Next month is November.

3. My birthday is in November.

4. It's on November 24th.

F Listen to Bill's story. Circle the correct word.

1-68

1. It's ____ .	a. April	b. August
2. Next month is ____ .	a. March	b. May
3. My birthday is in ____ .	a. July	b. August
4. It's on ____ .	a. July 15th	b. July 10th

Bill

3 Write about your birthday

A Write about the months. Complete the sentences. Use your own information.

It's _____ .

Next month is _____ .

My birthday is in _____ .

It's on _____ .

> **WRITER'S NOTE**
> Use *in* with months:
> <u>in</u> January
> <u>in</u> July
>
> Use *on* with dates:
> <u>on</u> January 1st
> <u>on</u> July 4th

B Read your story to a partner.

AT WORK ▶ Talk about day and night shifts

A Look at Kevin's work schedule. What color are day shifts? What color are night shifts?

☀ = day shift

🌙 = night shift

B Look at Kevin's work schedule. Listen to the questions. Write on the schedule.

1-69

▶▶ **TEST YOURSELF**

Talk to two partners. Write their names and birthdays.

Partner 1 Name: _____ Birthday: _____

Partner 2 Name: _____ Birthday: _____

1 Learn about *on* and *at*

A Look at the picture. Read the sentences.

The party is on Tuesday, July 4th. It's at 7:00.

B Study the form. Read the chart. Listen and repeat.

1-70

On and *At*				
The party is		Tuesday, July 4th		7:00.
The birthday party is	on	Saturday	at	5:30.
The class party is		September 3rd		9 p.m.

C Listen. Circle *on* or *at*.

1-71

1. on   at   5. on   at
2. on   at   6. on   at
3. on   at   7. on   at
4. on   at   8. on   at

D Complete the sentences. Circle *on* or *at*. Then read the sentences with a partner.

1. The 4th of July party is _____ Tuesday.   on   at
2. The birthday party is _____ 6:00.   on   at
3. The class party is _____ October 12th.   on   at
4. My birthday party is _____ Sunday.   on   at

ACADEMIC

2 Ask information and *yes/no* questions

A Listen. What time is the party?
1-72

Abena: <u>When</u> is the party?

Gloria: It's on Tuesday.

Abena: <u>Where</u> is the party?

Gloria: It's at my house.

Abena: <u>What time</u> is the party?

Gloria: It's at 6:00.

Abena: Are you excited?

Gloria: Yes, I am!

B Listen again. Complete the questions.
1-72

1. **Abena:** _____ is the party?

   Gloria: It's on Tuesday.

2. **Abena:** _____ is the party?

   Gloria: It's at my house.

3. **Abena:** _____ is the party?

   Gloria: It's at 6:00.

4. **Abena:** _____ you excited?

   Gloria: Yes, I am!

C Read the invitation for another party. Answer the questions. Circle *a* or *b*.

1. When is the birthday party?

   a. It's on Thursday.   b. It's at Pizza Town.

2. What time is the party?

   a. It's on Thursday.   b. It's at 6:00.

3. Where is the party?

   a. Yes, it is.   b. It's at Pizza Town.

4. Is the party on Thursday?

   a. Yes, it is.   b. It's at Pizza Town.

D Work with a partner. Read the questions and answers in 2C.

3 Ask and answer questions about dates and times

A Look at the pictures. Listen and repeat the words.

1-73

   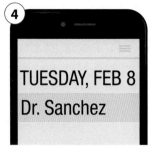

doctor   dentist   hairdresser   appointment

B Work with a partner. Ask and answer questions about the appointment cards and invitations.

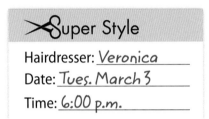
✂ Super Style
Hairdresser: *Veronica*
Date: *Tues. March 3*
Time: *6:00 p.m.*

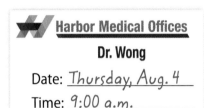
Harbor Medical Offices
Dr. Wong
Date: *Thursday, Aug. 4*
Time: *9:00 a.m.*

PARTY
Last day of school is June 14!
Class party at 12:00 p.m.
in Room 6!

🦷 APPOINTMENT CARD 🦷
Date: *Wednesday, June 14*
Time: *2:00 a.m. p.m.*
🦷 Family Dental Center Dr. David Golan

Claire's Birthday!
Friday, September 3rd at 5:00 p.m.
Pete's Café

New Year's Eve Party!
Dec. 31 8 p.m.-1 a.m.
618 Olive St.

A: When is the hairdresser appointment?

B: It's on March 3rd.

A: What time?

B: At 6:00.

A: Where?

B: At Super Style.

C Write sentences about two of the events in 3B.

The doctor appointment is on Thursday, August 4th at 9 a.m.

▶▶ TEST YOURSELF

Work with a partner. Ask and answer the questions.

When is your birthday?

What time are your classes?

Where is your English class?

1 Listen for important dates

1-74 **A** Look at the calendar. Listen and complete the dates.

Valley Adult School Calendar

Important Dates

Jan. 10	Registration
Jan. _____	first day of class
Jan. _____	Holiday (No classes!)
Mar. 27– _____	spring break (No classes!)
_____	last day of class

NEED HELP?

Martin Luther King Jr.'s birthday is a U.S. holiday. It is the third Monday in January.

B Answer the questions. Write the dates.

1. When is registration?   _January 10_
2. When is the first day of class?   _____
3. When is the first day of spring break?   _____
4. When is the last day of class?   _____

2 Practice your pronunciation

1-75 **A** Listen to the pronunciation of *t* and *th*.

See you **t**omorrow.   **Th**anks. See you **Th**ursday.

1-76 **B** Listen and repeat the words.

t	1. tomorrow	2. Tuesday	3. tired
th	4. Thursday	5. thirsty	6. thanks

1-77 **C** Listen. Check (✓) the sounds you hear.

	1.	2.	3.	4.	5.	6.
t	✓					
th						

3 Make conversation: say goodbye.

A Look at the pictures. Read the conversation.

B Listen and read.
1-78

Arun:	Goodbye. Have a nice weekend.
Oscar:	Thanks. You too. See you Monday.

Mrs. Robledo:	Bye. Have a nice break.
Tuan:	Thanks. You too. See you on the third.

C Listen again and repeat.
1-78

D Work with a partner. Practice the conversation. Use your own ideas.

A: Goodbye. Have a nice _____ .

B: Thanks. You too. See you _____ .

> **NEED HELP?**
>
> **Have a nice _____ .**
> holiday
> evening
> afternoon

▶▶ TEST YOURSELF

Talk to three classmates. Say hello and then say goodbye.
Use different ways to say goodbye.

1 Get ready to read

A Listen and repeat the years.

1-79

1. 1958	5. 2000
2. 1972	6. 2012
3. 1983	7. 2019
4. 1995	8. 2024

B Read the dates.

June 4, 2018 = 6/4/2018   July 12, 1990 = 7/12/1990

April 6, 2018 = 4/6/2018   December 7, 1990 = 12/7/1990

> **NEED HELP?**
>
> 6 / 4 / 2018
> month day   year

C Listen. Circle *a* or *b*.

1-80

1. a. 6/4/1999   (b.) 4/6/1999
2. a. 7/12/1960   b. 12/7/1960
3. a. 12/21/1982   b. 9/21/1982
4. a. 8/10/2017   b. 10/8/2017
5. a. 1/26/2013   b. 2/26/2013
6. a. 3/6/1951   b. 5/3/1951
7. a. 11/5/2015   b. 5/11/2015
8. a. 1/8/2019   b. 8/1/2019

D Work with a partner. Say the dates in 1C.

E Look at the pictures. Read the words.

garage

restaurant

hotel

F Ask and answer the questions with your classmates.

Do you work at a garage?

Do you work at a restaurant?

Do you work at a hotel?

2 Read a job application

A Read the job application.

EMPLOYMENT HISTORY

Company	Dates				Length of Time
	From		To		
Best Hotel	06 / 2015		12 / 2017		2 years, 6 months
	MM YYYY		MM YYYY		
Ed's Garage	09 / 2014		12 / 2014		3 months
	MM YYYY		MM YYYY		
Anne's Restaurant	11 / 2013		11 / 2014		1 year
	MM YYYY		MM YYYY		
General Store	08 / 2009		09 / 2012		3 years, 1 month
	MM YYYY		MM YYYY		

READING NOTE

MM = month

DD = day

YYYY = year

B Look at the job application. Write the dates. Use the names of the months.

1. General Store: from ___August 2009___ to _____ .
2. Anne's Restaurant: from _____ to _____ .
3. Ed's Garage: from _____ to _____ .
4. Best Hotel: from _____ to _____ .

C Do the math. Complete the job history. Use numbers and the words months and years.

EMPLOYMENT HISTORY

Company	Dates			To			Length of Time
	From						
CB's Bakery	02 / 01 / 2017			10 / 01 / 2017			*8 months*
	MM DD YYYY			MM DD YYYY			
Best Store	10 / 30 / 2015			10 / 30 / 2017			
	MM DD YYYY			MM DD YYYY			
Mike's Garage	07 / 10 / 2015			10 / 10 / 2017			
	MM DD YYYY			MM DD YYYY			

NEED HELP?

12 months = 1 year

16 months = 1 year, 4 months

 BRING IT TO LIFE

Find a job application on the Internet. Print it and bring it to class.

Circle two new words.

TEAMWORK & LANGUAGE REVIEW

A Work with a team. Talk about the calendar. Say what you see.

February

Sunday	Monday	Tuesday	Wednesday	Thursday	Friday	Saturday
30	31	1	2 Doctor appointment 2 p.m.	3	4	5
6	7	8	9	10	11 Class party 6:30 p.m.	12
13	14 Registration 9 a.m.– 5 p.m.	15	16	17	18	19 Jan's birthday party at Pizza Town 8 p.m.
20	21 No school!	22	23	24 Hairdresser 4 p.m.	25 Job Interview! Best Bakery	26
27	28	Presidents' Day is a U.S. holiday. It's the third Monday in February.				

B Look at the calendar. Complete the questions and answers.

1. **A:** When is Jan's birthday?
   B: It's on _____ .

2. **A:** What time is the class party?
   B: It's at _____ .

3. **A:** Where is the job interview?
   B: It's at _____ .

4. **A:** Is the class party on Friday?
   B: _____ .

5. **A:** _____ President's Day?
   B: It's on February 21st.

6. **A:** _____ the hairdresser appointment?
   B: It's at 4 p.m.

7. **A:** _____ the birthday party?
   B: It's at Pizza Town.

8. **A:** _____ registration?
   B: It's on Monday.

C Ask and answer questions about the calendar.

A: When is the birthday party?

B: It's on Saturday, February 19th. What time is registration?

C: It's at 9 a.m.

D Look at the calendar. Complete the sentences with the date and the time.

1. The doctor appointment is <u> on February 2nd at 2 p.m. </u> .

2. The class party is _____ .

3. Registration is _____ .

4. Jan's birthday party is _____ .

E Write two new sentences about the calendar.

1. _____

2. _____

PROBLEM SOLVING AT SCHOOL

A Listen. Look at the pictures.

1-81

Sharon's Problem

B Work with your classmates. Help Sharon.

a. Call the school.

b. Go to school now.

5 How Much Is It?

LESSON **1** VOCABULARY

1 Learn words for money

A Look at the pictures. Count the money.

B Listen and point to the pictures.
2-02

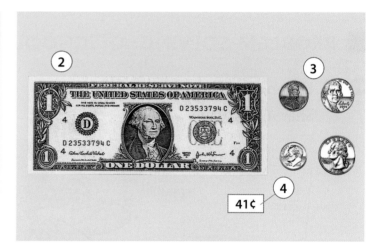

41¢

1¢ = $0.01

5¢ = $0.05

10¢ = $0.10

25¢ = $0.25

C Listen and repeat the words.
2-02

1. bills
2. dollar
3. coins
4. cents
5. penny
6. nickel
7. dime
8. quarter

D Say the new words with a partner.

E Work with a partner. Cover the words in 1C. Point to the pictures in 1B. Say the words.

2 Talk about money

A Look at the picture. Complete the words.

1. p __e__ __n__ n y
2. d i ___ e
3. b ___ ___ l s
4. ___ o l l ___ r

5. ___ ___ i n s
6. n i c ___ ___ l
7. ___ u a ___ t e r
8. c ___ ___ t s

B Copy the words from 2A in your notebook.

C Listen. Circle *a* or *b*.
2-03

1. a. 65¢   b. 75¢
2. a. $2   b. $0.12
3. a. 35¢   b. $35

4. a. $6   b. $16
5. a. $7   b. $0.07
6. a. 80¢   b. $0.08

D Listen and repeat.
2-04

1. **A:** How much is it?
   B: It's 25¢.

2. **A:** How much is it?
   B: It's $6.

E Work with a partner. Point to the money in 2A. Practice the conversation.

A: How much is it?

B: It's _____ .

▶▶ TEST YOURSELF

Work with a partner. Ask and answer the questions.

How much is a quarter? How much is a nickel? How much is a dime?
How much is a penny? How much is a dollar?

1 Learn about shopping

A Look at the picture. Say the numbers.

B Listen and repeat the words.

2-05

1. price
2. pants
3. shirt
4. jacket
5. sweater

6. socks
7. shoes
8. clothes
9. cheap
10. expensive

C Complete the sentences with the words from 1B.

1. Shirts, sweaters, and pants are ___clothes___ .
2. The _____ is $32.
3. The _____ are $6.99.
4. The _____ of the shirts is $24.99.
5. Those shoes are $10.99. They're _____ .
6. The _____ are $17.
7. The _____ are $24.99.
8. Those _____ are $165.99. They're _____ !

2 Prepare to write: shopping

A Look at the pictures. Listen and read the sentences. Where do you want to shop?

The clerks are friendly.
The prices are low.

The clerks aren't friendly.
The prices are high.

B Listen and repeat the words.

1. clerk
2. friendly
3. high
4. low

C Listen and read Daniela's story.

1. I shop at Clothes Mart.
2. The clerks are friendly.
3. The clothes are good.
4. The prices are low.

> **WRITER'S NOTE**
>
> Use capital letters for names of places.
>
> **C**lothes **M**art
> **S**uper **S**hoes

Ken

D Listen to Ken's story. Circle the correct word.
2-09

1. I shop at _____ World.   a. Shirt   b. Shoe
2. The _____ are good.   a. shoes   b. sweaters
3. The clerks are _____ .   a. cheap   b. friendly
4. The _____ are low.   a. pants   b. prices

3 Write about shopping

A Write about shopping. Complete the sentences. Use your own ideas.

I shop at _____ .

The _____ are good.

The clerks are _____ .

The prices are _____ .

B Read your story to a partner.

AT WORK ▶ **Calculate sale prices**

A Look at the picture. Say the prices.

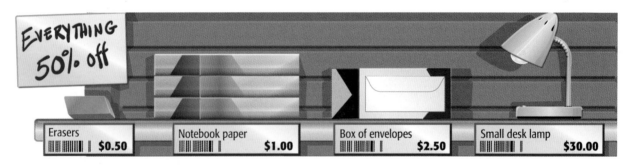

EVERYTHING 50% off

| Erasers | Notebook paper | Box of envelopes | Small desk lamp |
| $0.50 | $1.00 | $2.50 | $30.00 |

B Do the math. Write the sale price.

1. $0.50 × 0.5 = $ _0.25_   An eraser is $ _0.25_ .

2. $1.00 × 0.5 = $_____   The paper is $_____ .

3. $2.50 × 0.5 = $_____   The envelopes are $_____ .

4. $30.00 × 0.5 = $_____   A lamp is $_____ .

NEED HELP?

50% = ½ = 0.50
(Fifty percent equals one half)

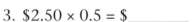 **TEST YOURSELF**

Work with a partner. Write sentences about the picture in A.

The _____ is cheap. The _____ are $ _____ . The prices are _____ .

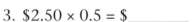

1 Use *This* and *That*

A Look at the pictures. How many shirts do you see?

This sweater is $35.

That sweater is $42.

This shirt is $22.

That shirt is $54.

B Listen and repeat the sentences.

2-10

C Look at the sentences in 1A. When do we say *that*?

D Look at the pictures. Circle *a* or *b*. Then read the sentences with a partner.

1. _____ sweater is $12.
   a. This   b. That

3. _____ dictionary is $5.99.
   a. This   b. That

2. _____ sweater is $9.99.
   a. This   b. That

4. _____ dictionary is $16.
   a. This   b. That

2 Use *These* and *Those*

A Look at the pictures. Listen and repeat the sentences.

2-11

<u>These</u> pants are $14.   <u>Those</u> pants are $45.

B Match the pictures with the sentences.

__*b*__ 1. These pants are $45.   ____ 4. Those shoes are $34.50.

____ 2. Those pants are $45.   ____ 5. These pens are $3.99.

____ 3. These shoes are $34.50   ____ 6. Those pens are $3.99.

C Complete the sentences. Circle *a* or *b*.

1. ____ pencil is 25¢.   4. ____ notebooks are cheap.
   a. This   b. These   a. This   b. These

2. ____ shoes are $30.   5. ____ chairs are $49.99.
   a. That   b. Those   a. That   b. Those

3. ____ clock is expensive.   6. ____ binder is 99¢.
   a. That   b. Those   a. This   b. These

D Work with a partner. Read the sentences in 2B and 2C.

3 Talk about prices

A Look at the pictures. Listen and repeat the words.

2-12

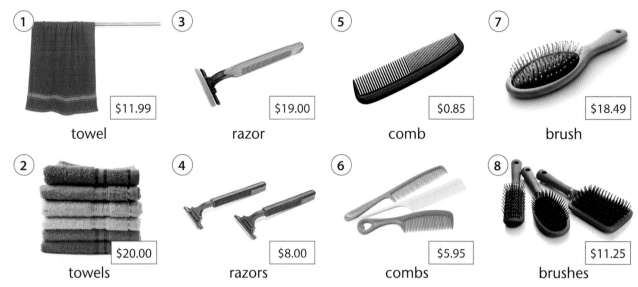

1. towel — $11.99
3. razor — $19.00
5. comb — $0.85
7. brush — $18.49

2. towels — $20.00
4. razors — $8.00
6. combs — $5.95
8. brushes — $11.25

B Work with a partner. Point to the pictures in 3A in your own book. Ask and answer questions about the prices. Use *this* and *these*.

Clerk: How much is this towel?
Customer: It's $11.99.
Clerk: How much are these towels?
Customer: They're $20.

C Work with a partner. Point to your partner's book. Ask and answer questions about the prices. Use *that* and *those*.

Clerk: How much is that towel?
Customer: It's $11.99.
Clerk: How much are those towels?
Customer: They're $20.

D Write sentences about three pictures in 3A.

That towel is $ 11.99.

▶▶ TEST YOURSELF

Look the picture on page 62, 1A. Write three sentences about the picture. Use *that* and *those*.

Those pants are $ 17.

_____

_____

1 Listen for amounts

A Look at the money. What coins do you see?

🔊 **B** Listen. Circle *a* or *b*.
2-13

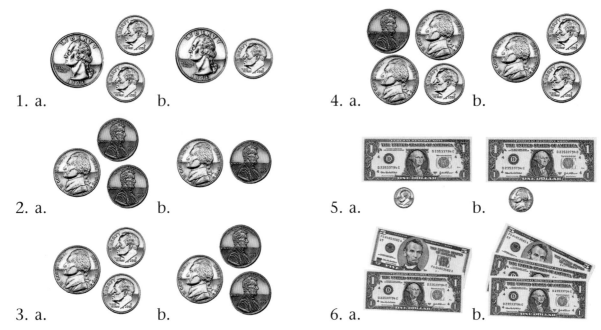

1. a.   b.   4. a.   b.

2. a.   b.   5. a.   b.

3. a.   b.   6. a.   b.

C Talk to your partner. Point to the pictures in 1A. Say the amounts.

It's 45¢.

2 Practice your pronunciation

🔊 **A** Listen for *s* and *sh* sounds.
2-14

s	1. socks	2. sweater	3. Sunday	4. September
sh	5. shoes	6. shirt	7. shop	8. she

🔊 **B** Listen and check (✓) the sounds you hear.
2-15

	1.	2.	3.	4.	5.
s	✓				
sh					

🔊 **C** Listen again and repeat.
2-15

3 Make conversation: talk about prices

A Look at the pictures. Read the conversation.

B Listen and read.

2-16

George: Is this shirt on sale?

Kumi: No, it's not.

George: How about these shoes?

Kumi: They're 50% off.

George: Great!

C Listen again and repeat.

2-16

D Work with a partner. Practice the conversation. Use your own ideas.

A: Is this _____ on sale?

B: No, it's not.

A: How about these _____ ?

B: They're _____ .

A: Great!

NEED HELP?

sweater   brush

pencils   socks

▶▶ TEST YOURSELF

Talk to your classmates. Ask and answer questions about things in your classroom.

A: Is this pencil on sale?

B: Yes. It's 50% off.

A: How much is that dictionary?

B: It's $15.

1 Get ready to read

A Look at the pictures. Listen and repeat.

2-17

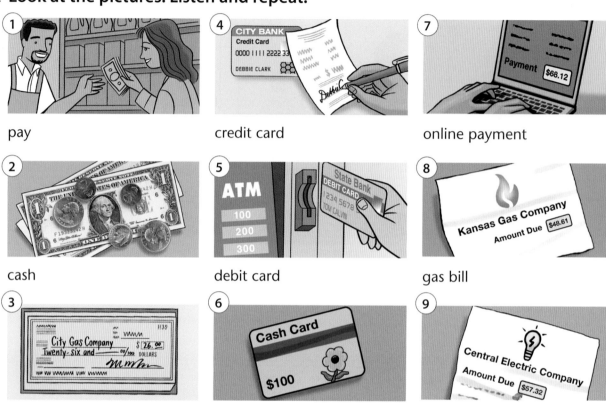

1. pay

2. cash

3. check

4. credit card

5. debit card

6. pre-paid card

7. online payment

8. gas bill

9. electric bill

B Listen. Circle *a* or *b*.

2-18

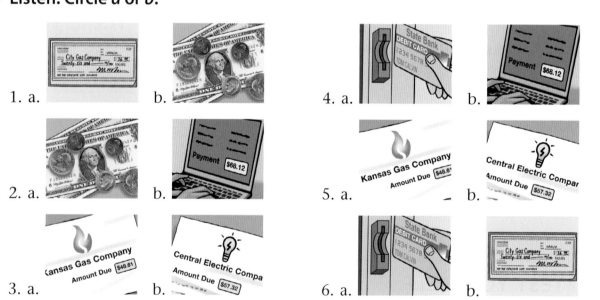

1. a.   b.

2. a.   b.

3. a.   b.

4. a.   b.

5. a.   b.

6. a.   b.

C Are your bills *high* or *low*? Complete the sentences

1. My gas bill is _____ .
2. My electric bill is _____ .
3. I like to pay with _____ .

2 Read about ways to pay

A Read the sentences and the pie chart.

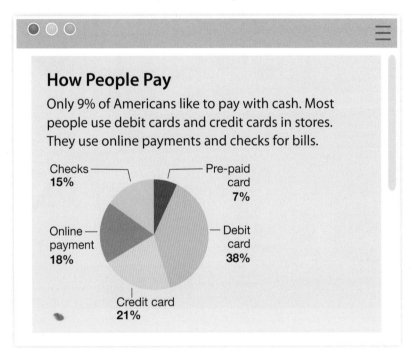

How People Pay

Only 9% of Americans like to pay with cash. Most people use debit cards and credit cards in stores. They use online payments and checks for bills.

Checks 15%
Pre-paid card 7%
Online payment 18%
Debit card 38%
Credit card 21%

READING NOTE

A pie chart shows **percent**.

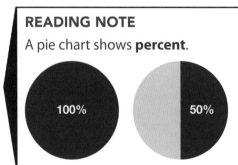

100% 50%

Source: *CreditCards.com*

B Listen and read the sentences again.

2-19

C Look at the sentences and the pie chart. Circle *a* or *b*.

1. Most Americans use _____ cards in stores.

   a. debit   b. pre-paid

2. Most people pay their bills with _____ .

   a. cash   b. an online payment

3. Only _____ of people use pre-paid cards.

   a. 9%   b. 7%

4. _____ of people write checks.

   a. 15%   b. 50%

⏻ BRING IT TO LIFE

Look at a bill at home. Circle one new word.

Copy the word in your notebook.

A Work with a team. Talk about the picture. Say what you see.

B Write the words you know in the chart.

Clothes	People	Other

C Look up three words you don't know in a dictionary. Add them to the chart.

D Talk about the picture. Use *this*, *that*, *these* and *those*.

These sweaters are cheap.

E Look at the picture. Complete the sentences. Use the words in the box.

| is | friendly | ~~much~~ | on sale | expensive | prices |

1. How ___much___ are the pants?
2. The _____ are low.
3. The men's shoes are _____ .
4. The sweaters are _____ .
5. That sweater _____ $15.
6. The clerk is _____ .

F Write two new sentences about the picture.

1. _____
2. _____

PROBLEM SOLVING

A Listen. Look at the pictures.

2-20

Ivan's Problem

B Work with your classmates. Help Ivan.

a. Ask for a dime. b. Go home. c. Buy cheaper shoes.

UNIT

6

A LOOK AT
■ Family members
■ The simple present
■ Employee information form

That's My Son

LESSON **1** VOCABULARY

1 Learn about friends and family

A Look at the pictures. Count the men and women.

🔊 **B** Listen and point to the pictures.
2-21

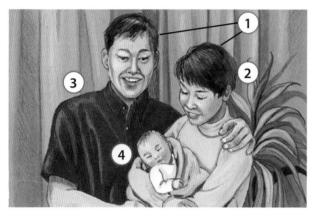 

🔊 **C** Listen and repeat the words.
2-21

1. parents	4. baby	7. friend
2. mother	5. girl	8. husband
3. father	6. boy	9. wife

D Say the new words with a partner.

E Work with a partner. Cover the words. Point to the pictures.
Say the words.

2 Talk about families

A Look at the picture. Complete the words.

1. w ___ f ____
2. h ___ s ___ a n d
3. ___ a ___ h e r
4. p ___ r e n t ___
5. m ___ t h e ___
6. b a ___ y
7. b ___ y
8. ___ i r l
9. f r i ___ ___ d

B Copy the words from 2A in your notebook.

C Listen and repeat.

2-22

1. **A:** Is this the father?
   B: No, that's the mother.

2. **A:** Is this the boy?
   B: Yes, that's the boy.

D Work with a partner. Point to the people in 2A. Practice the conversations.

A: Is this the _____ ?
B: No, that's the _____ .

A: Is this the _____ ?
B: Yes, that's the _____ .

▶▶ TEST YOURSELF

Use your notebook. Copy the chart.
Write three words in each column.

father

1 Learn about marital status

2-23

A Read and listen to the sentences. Are they using first names or last names in titles?

Marital Status

We're married.　　　　I'm single.　　　　We're divorced.

Titles

I'm Mr. Jain.　I'm Mr. Cohen.　I'm Mrs. Kim.　I'm Miss Diaz.　I'm Ms. Lim.　I'm Ms. Rios.
I'm single.　　I'm married.　　I'm married.　　I'm single.　　I'm single.　　I'm married.

B Choose the correct marital status. Circle one or two answers.

1. **Mr.**　　a. married　　b. single　　　3. **Ms.**　　a. married　　b. single

2. **Mrs.**　　a. married　　b. single　　　4. **Miss**　　a. married　　b. single

C Listen. Circle *a* or *b*.
2-24

1. a. I'm Mr. Jones.　　b. I'm Mrs. Jones.

2. a. I'm Mr. Wong.　　b. I'm Miss Wong.

3. a. I'm Mrs. Park.　　b. I'm Ms. Park.

4. a. I'm Mrs. Chavez.　　b. I'm Mr. Chavez.

D Talk to your classmates. Introduce yourself.
Use your title and last name.

Hello. I'm Mrs. _____ .

Nice to meet you. I'm Mr. _____ .

2 Prepare to write: family information

A Look at the picture. Point to the girls.

B Listen and repeat the words.
2-25

1. children
2. child
3. daughter
4. son
5. brother
6. sister

C Listen and read Mrs. Mota's story.
2-26

1. These are my children.
2. This is my son.
3. He's seven years old.
4. This is my daughter.
5. She's ten years old.

WRITER'S NOTE

Write sentences.

Use a capital letter for the first word.

Use a period (.) after the last word.

These are my friends.

D Complete the sentences with the words from 2B.

1. Mrs. Mota has two _____ . They are Moira and David.
2. Mrs. Mota has one _____ . Her name is Moira.
3. Mrs. Mota has one _____ . His name is David.
4. Moira and David are brother and _____ .

E Listen to Mr. Awad's story. Write the correct word.

2-27

1. These are my _____children_____ .
2. Fadi is my _____ .
3. He's _____ years old.
4. Naja is my _____ .
5. She's _____ years old.

3 Write about your family or friends

A Write about your family or friends. Copy and complete the sentences. Show or draw a picture.

This is my _____ . He's _____ years old.

This is my _____ . She's _____ years old.

B Read your story to a partner.

AT WORK ▶ Complete an employee information form

A Read the employee information forms.

Name: **Eric Wang**
EMERGENCY CONTACT INFORMATION
name: **Jill Wang**
relationship: **wife**
phone number:
587-555-8971

Name: **Colin Ward**
EMERGENCY CONTACT INFORMATION
name: **Kelly Gomez**
relationship: **sister**
phone number:
701-555-5098

Name: **Maria Kane**
EMERGENCY CONTACT INFORMATION
name: **Paul Kane**
relationship: **father**
phone number:
891-555-1295

B Complete the form.

Name: _____
EMERGENCY CONTACT INFORMATION

_____ _____ _____
　　　　　name　　　　　　　　　　relationship　　　　　　　　phone number

▶▶ TEST YOURSELF

Copy the sentences. Close your book. Then complete the sentences. Use your own ideas.

My _____ is _____ years old.　　My _____ is _____ years old.

1 Use possessive adjectives

🔊 **A** **Look at the pictures. Listen and read the sentences.**

2-28

I'm a student. <u>My</u> name is Marie.

You're my friend. <u>Your</u> name is Silvia.

He's my brother. <u>His</u> name is Claude.

She's my sister. <u>Her</u> name is Brigitte.

They're my coworkers. <u>Their</u> names are Annie and Donna.

We're married. <u>Our</u> names are Mr. And Mrs. Laurent.

B **Look at the underlined words. Which ones are plural?**

C **Complete the sentences. Circle *a* or *b*.**

1. I'm a student. ____ name is Catherine.
   a. Your   ⓑ. My

2. He's my son. ____ name is Ricky.
   a. My   b. His

3. She's my mother. ____ name is Lonnie.
   a. His   b. Her

4. You're my friend. ____ name is Bette.
   a. Your   b. My

5. They're my coworkers. ____ names are Peg and Thinh.
   a. Her   b. Their

6. We're parents. ____ names are Mr. and Mrs. Bishop.
   a. Our   b. Their

D **Work with a partner. Read the sentences in 1C.**

AT WORK

2 Learn about the simple present

A Look at the pictures. Read the sentences.

He lives in California. She lives in New York. He lives in Texas. They live in Florida.

B Study the form. Read the charts. Listen and repeat.

2-29

The Simple Present		
Affirmative Statements		
I You We They	live	in New York.
He She	lives	

C Complete the sentences. Circle *a* or *b*.

1. I ____ in Nevada.
   (a.) live   b. lives
2. He ____ in Washington.
   a. live   b. lives
3. She ____ in Oregon.
   a. live   b. lives
4. They ____ in California.
   a. live   b. lives

D Complete the sentences with *live* or *lives*.

1. My brother ___lives___ in Oregon.

2. My sisters _____ in Nevada.

3. My parents _____ in Korea.

4. My son _____ in Guatemala.

5. My mother and father _____ in Nicaragua.

6. My children _____ in Arizona.

E Work with a partner. Talk about your family.

My _____ lives in _____ .

My _____ and _____ live in _____ .

3 Talk about names and places

A Look at the friends' list. Listen and repeat the sentences.

2-30

Your Friends (United States)

Mick — Washington

Maria / Kai — Montana

Ned / Sara — Nebraska

Lin — Texas

Jill — Michigan

John — Maine

Sid — Ohio

Tia — Colorado

Al / Phil — North Carolina

Jin — New York

Nan — Georgia

Zack — Florida

1. His name is Mick. He lives in Washington.
2. Their names are Maria and Kai. They live in Montana.

B Work with a partner. Talk about the people in 3A. Use *he, she,* and *they*.

Her name is Tia. She lives in Colorado.

Their names are Maria and Kai. They live in Montana.

C Write sentences about three of the people in 3A.

Her name is Tia. She lives in Colorado.

Their names are Maria and Kai. They live in Montana.

▸▸ TEST YOURSELF

Talk to three classmates. Tell them about your friends and family.

My friend lives in San Francisco. Her name is Kara.

1 Listen for height

A Look at the ruler. How many inches are there?

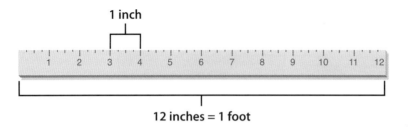

1 inch

12 inches = 1 foot

B Listen. Write the heights

2-31

1. How tall is her son?

   He's __5__ feet and ____ inches tall.

2. How tall is her daughter?

   She's ____ feet and ____ inches tall.

Jon   Katy

2 Practice your pronunciation

A Listen for *who* and *how*.

2-32

Who	How
1. Who is he?	4. How are you?
2. Who is she?	5. How old is he?
3. Who are they?	6. How tall is she?

B Listen for *who* and *how*. Check (✓) the correct column.

2-33

	1.	2.	3.	4.	5.	6.
Who						
How	✓					

C Listen again and repeat.

2-33

3 Make conversation: talk about families and friends

A Look at the pictures. Read the conversation.

B Listen and read.

2-34

Chang Sun: Who's that?

Nancy: That's my daughter. She lives in Houston.

Chang Sun: How old is she?

Nancy: She's 5. Who's that?

Chang Sun: That's my father.

Nancy: What's his name?

Chang Sun: His name is Lee. He lives in Houston too.

C Listen again and repeat.

2-34

D Work with a partner. Practice the conversation. Use your own ideas.

A: Who's that?

B: That's my _____ .

A: What's _____ name?

B: _____ name is _____ . He/she lives in _____ .

▶▶ TEST YOURSELF

Look at the pictures on page 77. Ask and answer questions about Mrs. Mota's children.

Who is ____ ?   What's ____ name ?   How old is ____ ?

1 Get ready to read

A Look at the chart.

Age	Grades		School
5–6 years old	Kindergarten		Elementary school
6–11 years old	First grade Second grade	Third grade Fourth grade	Elementary school
	Fifth grade		Elementary or middle school
11–14 years old	Sixth grade		Elementary or middle school
	Seventh grade	Eighth grade	Middle or junior high school
14–18 years old	Ninth grade Tenth grade	Eleventh grade Twelfth grade	High school

B Complete the sentences. Circle *a* or *b*.

1. His daughter is eight years old. She's in ____ grade.

   a. eighth   b. third

2. Her son is five years old. He's in ____ .

   a. fifth grade   b. kindergarten

3. Their son is in the third grade. He's in ____ .

   a. elementary school b. high school

4. My daughter is in eleventh grade. She's ____ years old.

   a. eleven   b. seventeen

C Look at the pictures. Read the words.

 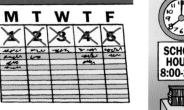  

come   every day   on time   do homework

D Check (✓) the sentences about you.

- ☐ I come to class every day.
- ☐ I come to class on time.
- ☐ I do my homework.

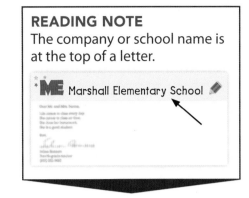

READING NOTE
The company or school name is at the top of a letter.

2 Read a note

A Read the note from the teacher.

Marshall Elementary School ✏️

Dear Mr. and Mrs. Santos,

Lila comes to class every day.
She comes to class on time.
She does her homework.
She is a good student.

Best,

Selma Romero
Selma Romero
Fourth-grade teacher
(832) 555-9982

🔊 B Listen and read the note again.

2-35

C Look at the note. Circle *a* or *b*.

1. Lila is in _____ .
   a. third grade
   b. fourth grade

2. Ms. Romero is the _____
   a. mother
   b. teacher

3. Mrs. Santos is the _____ .
   a. mother
   b. father

4. Lila is in _____ .
   a. middle school
   b. elementary school

 BRING IT TO LIFE

Find the names of the elementary school, middle school (or junior high), and high school in your community. Tell the class.

TEAMWORK & LANGUAGE REVIEW

A Work with a team. Talk about the picture. Say what you see.

B Write the words you know in the chart.

Family		Other
Male	**Female**	**Other**

C Look up three words you don't know in a dictionary.
Add them to the chart.

D Look at the picture. Complete the sentence with the words
son, friend, baby, daughter, or *father.*

1. The _____baby_____ is 9 months old. _____ name is John.
2. The _____ is 15 years old. _____ name is Dina.
3. The _____ is 6 years old. _____ name is Denis.
4. Ivan is the _____ . Lee is his _____ .

E Write two more sentences about the picture.

1. _____
2. _____

PROBLEM SOLVING AT HOME

A Listen. Look at the pictures.

2-36

Rosa's Problem

B Work with your classmates. Help Rosa.

a. Say, "No more baseball."

b. Say, "Only play baseball on Saturday."

c. Talk to the teacher.

UNIT

7 Do You Need Apples?

A LOOK AT
- Food
- The simple present
- Supermarket job ads

LESSON **1** VOCABULARY

1 Learn about fruit and vegetables

A Look at the pictures. Say the prices.

B Listen and point to the pictures.
2-37

C Listen and repeat the words.
2-37

1. fruit	4. grapes	7. broccoli
2. bananas	5. oranges	8. cabbage
3. apples	6. vegetables	9. corn

D Say the new words with a partner.

E Work with a partner. Cover the word. Point to the pictures in 1B. Say the words.

2 Talk about fruit and vegetables

A Look at the picture. Complete the words.

1. b a n ___ ___ ___ s
2. ___ r ___ p e s
3. o ___ a n g e ___
4. ___ p ___ l e s
5. ___ r u ___ t

6. ___ o ___ n
7. b r o c c ___ ___ i
8. c a b ___ ___ ___ e
9. ___ ___ g e ___ a b l e s

B Copy the words from 2A in your notebook.

C Listen and repeat.

2-38

1. Where are the apples?
2. Where are the bananas?
3. Where are the grapes?
4. Where are the vegetables?

5. Where is the broccoli?
6. Where is the cabbage?
7. Where is the corn?
8. Where is the fruit?

D Work with a partner. Ask the questions in 2C. Point to the fruit and vegetables in 2A and answer the questions.

A: Where are the apples?

B: They're right here.

A: Where is the broccoli?

B: It's right here.

▶▶ TEST YOURSELF

Use your notebook. Copy the chart. Write words for fruit and vegetables.

Fruit	Vegetables
apples	

1 Learn about more food groups

A Look at the pictures. Listen and repeat the words.
2-39

1. cheese

4. bread

7. beef

2. eggs

5. chicken

8. lamb

3. milk

6. pork

9. rice

B Work with your class. Write one more word in each box.

Meat	Dairy	Grains	Fruit	Vegetables
pork	milk	bread	apples	broccoli

C Listen to the food groups. Circle *a* or *b*.
2-40

1. a. pork
   b. broccoli

2. a. oranges
   b. lamb

3. a. grapes
   b. corn

4. a. cabbage
   b. chicken

5. a. beef
   b. milk

6. a. rice
   b. eggs

2 Prepare to write: food I like

A Look at the pictures. What food do you see?

Barbara

B Listen and read Barbara's story.

2-41

1. I like cheese.
2. I don't like pork.
3. My husband likes beef.
4. My daughter likes chicken.
5. We all like rice.

C Talk to a partner. Talk about the food you like and don't like in each food group.

A: I like all vegetables.

B: I like broccoli and corn. I don't like cabbage.

A: I like chicken and pork.

B: I don't like meat.

D Listen to Don's story. Circle the correct word.

1. I like ____ .   a. meat   b. milk
2. I don't like ____ .   a. chicken   b. cheese
3. My wife likes ____ .   a. lamb   b. rice
4. My son likes ____ .   a. rice   b. eggs

Don

3 Write about food you like

A Complete the sentences. Copy them in your notebook.

I like _____ .

I don't like _____ .

My _____ likes _____ .

My _____ likes _____ .

> **WRITER'S NOTE**
> Check your work.
> • Do sentences have a capital letter and a period?
> • Is the spelling correct?

B Read your story to a partner.

AT WORK ▶ Read supermarket job ads

A Read the job ads and complete the chart.

Jobs at Sam's Market

1. bagger	2. manager	3. cashier
Weekends, 5–11 p.m.	Tues.–Sat., 4 p.m.–12 a.m.	Mon.,Wed., Fri. 7 a.m.–3 p.m.

	work on Saturdays	work in the evening	work on Wednesday	work in the morning
bagger	✓			
manager	✓			
cashier				

B Talk to your classmates. Are these good jobs?

▶▶ TEST YOURSELF

Write three sentences about things you like and don't like.

I like _____ .   I don't like _____ .

1 Use negative statements with the simple present

A Look at the pictures. What food do you see?

He likes rice and vegetables.
He doesn't like meat.

She likes bananas.
She doesn't like cabbage.

They like chicken.
They don't like rice.

B Study the form. Read the chart. Listen and repeat.

2-43

The Simple Present		
Negative Statements		
I You We They	don't like	cabbage.
He She	doesn't like	

C Complete the sentences. Use *don't like* or *doesn't like*.

1. He _____ chicken.

3. She _____ fruit.

2. He _____ milk.

4. They _____ vegetables.

Use the simple present to express likes, dislikes, and needs   **93**

2 Learn about *yes/no* questions with the simple present

A Look at the pictures. Listen and read the conversations.

2-44

A: <u>Do you need</u> rice?

B: Yes, <u>I do</u>.

A: <u>Do you need</u> bread?

B: No, <u>I don't</u>.

A: <u>Do they need</u> oranges?

B: Yes, <u>they do</u>.

A: <u>Do they need</u> apples?

B: No, <u>they don't</u>.

A: <u>Does he need</u> milk?

B: Yes, <u>he does</u>.

A: <u>Does he need</u> eggs?

B: No, <u>he doesn't</u>.

A: <u>Do we need</u> broccoli?

B: Yes, <u>we do</u>.

A: <u>Do we need</u> cabbage?

B: No, <u>we don't</u>.

B Look at the picture. Complete the questions. Use *does* and *doesn't*.

1. **A:** _____ he need rice?

   B: Yes, he _____ .

2. **A:** _____ he need chicken?

   B: No, he _____ .

□ rice
□ grapes
□ cabbage
□ eggs

C Look at the picture. Complete the questions. Use *do* and *don't*.

1. **A:** _____ they need bread?

   B: Yes, they _____ .

2. **A:** _____ they need beef?

   B: No, they _____ .

□ bread
□ cheese
□ lamb
□ corn

D Work with a partner. Read the questions and answers in 2B and 2C. Ask one more question about each picture.

A: Does he need _____ ?

B: _____ .

A: Do they need _____ ?

B: _____ .

3 Ask about likes and needs

A Listen and repeat.

2-45

1. **A:** Do you like oranges?

   B: Yes, I do.

2. **A:** Do you like lamb?

   B: No, I don't.

B Work with a partner. Talk about the food in the pictures. Practice the conversation.

A: Do you like _____ ?

B: _____ .

C Look at the pictures. Listen and repeat the conversations.

2-46

1. **A:** Does he need eggs?

   B: Yes, he does.

2. **A:** Does she need apples?

   B: No, she doesn't.

D Talk to a partner. Look at the pictures in 3C. Practice the conversation.

A: Does _____ need _____ ?

B: _____ .

E Write three sentences about the pictures in 3C. Use *needs* and *doesn't need*.

He needs eggs. He doesn't need pork.

▶▶ TEST YOURSELF

Write one sentence about a picture in 2A.

She needs rice.
She doesn't need bread.

1 Listen for prices

A Listen and point to the food.

2-47

UNITED SUPERMARKET **SALE!**

apples   oranges   grapes   bananas

_____ a **pound**   _____ a **pound**   _____ a **pound**   _____ a **pound**

B Listen again. Write the prices in the ad in 1A.

2-47

C Look at the ads. Do the math.

Apples   3 lbs. for $2

Oranges   5 lbs. for $3

> **NEED HELP?**
>
> lb. = pound
> lbs. = pounds

1. Jane needs 6 pounds of apples.

   3 lbs. × 2 = 6 lbs.

   $2 × 2 = $ _4_

   6 lbs. of apples = $____

2. Azim needs 10 pounds of oranges.

   5 lbs. × ____ = 10 lbs.

   $3 × 2 = $____

   10 lbs. of oranges = $_____

2 Practice your pronunciation

A Listen for final *s*.

2-48

-s	1. apples	2. bananas	3. pens
-es	4. oranges	5. peaches	6. classes

B Listen. Check (✓) the final sound you hear.

2-49

	1.	2.	3.	4.	5.
-s					
-es	✓				

> **NEED HELP?**
>
>
>
> peaches

C Listen again and repeat.

2-49

3 Make conversation: ask for help in a store

A Look at the pictures. Read the conversation.

B Listen and read.

Clerk: Can I help you?

Rosita: Yes, I need apples.

Clerk: Here you go. They're $2 a pound.

Rosita: Thanks.

Clerk: You're welcome.

C Listen again and repeat.

D Work with a partner. Practice the conversation. Use the ad in 1A.

A: Can I help you?

B: Yes, I need _____ .

A: Here you go. They're _____ .

B: Thanks.

A: You're welcome.

▶▶ TEST YOURSELF

Talk to your classmates. Role-play a clerk and a customer.
Talk about the food on page 90. Point to the pictures.

Clerk: Can I help you?

Customer: Yes, I need _____ .

Clerk: Here you go.

Customer: Thanks.

1 Get ready to read

A Look at the pictures. Listen and repeat.

2-51

1 a can of coffee

2 a can of soup

3 a bottle of water

4 a bottle of juice

5 a box of cereal

6 a box of tea

B Listen. Circle *a* or *b*.

2-52

1. a. can   b. bottle   4. a. can   b. bottle
2. a. bottle   b. box   5. a. box   b. bottle
3. a. can   b. bottle   6. a. box   b. can

C Look at the pictures. Read the words.

buy

shopping

candy

D Check (✓) the sentence about you.

☐ I like shopping.

☐ I don't like shopping.

2 Read a shopping list

A Read the shopping list.

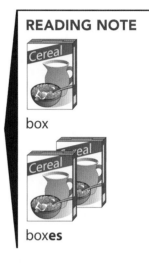

READING NOTE

box

box**es**

B Look at the shopping list. Circle *True* or *False*.

1. They need two cans of soup.	(True)	False
2. They need cabbage.	True	False
3. They need two boxes of cereal.	True	False
4. They need fruit.	True	False
5. They need a box of tea.	True	False
6. They need two bottles of orange juice.	True	False
7. They need one can of coffee.	True	False
8. They need candy.	True	False

NEED HELP?

True = ✓
False = ✗

 BRING IT TO LIFE

Look at a supermarket website.
Talk about the food you need.

TEAMWORK & LANGUAGE REVIEW

ACADEMIC

A Work with a team. Talk about the picture. Say what you see.

David

Paula

B Write the words you know in the chart.

Fruit	Vegetables	Grains	Meat	Other

C Look up three words you don't know in a dictionary. Add them to the chart.

D Complete the questions and answers. Use *do, don't, does,* or *doesn't.*

1. A: _Does_ David like broccoli?

   B: Yes, he does.

2. A: _____ David and Paula need milk?

   B: No, they _____ .

3. A: _____ they like juice?

   B: No, they _____ .

4. A: _____ they need rice?

   B: No, they _____ .

5. A: _____ Paula like vegetables?

   B: Yes, she _____ .

6. A: _____ David like cereal?

   B: No, he _____ .

E Read the questions and answers in D. Write two sentences about David and Paula.

David likes broccoli.   David and Paula don't need milk.

1. _____

2. _____

PROBLEM SOLVING IN DAILY LIFE

A Listen. Look at the pictures.

2-53

Duncan's Problem

6 a.m.   12 p.m.   8 p.m.   10 p.m.

B Work with your classmates. Help Duncan.

a. Eat breakfast at home.   b. Make lunch.   c. Walk to work.

UNIT

8 What's the Matter?

A LOOK AT
- Health
- *Have* and *has*
- Reporting sickness

LESSON 1 VOCABULARY

1 Learn parts of the body

A Look at the picture. Is she sick?

B Listen and point to the picture.

2-54

C Listen and repeat the words.

2-54

1. head	3. ear	5. arm	7. hand	9. foot
2. eye	4. nose	6. stomach	8. leg	10. back

D Say the new words with a partner.

E Work with a partner. Cover the words. Point to the picture. Say the words.

2 Talk about parts of the body

A Look at the picture. Complete the words.

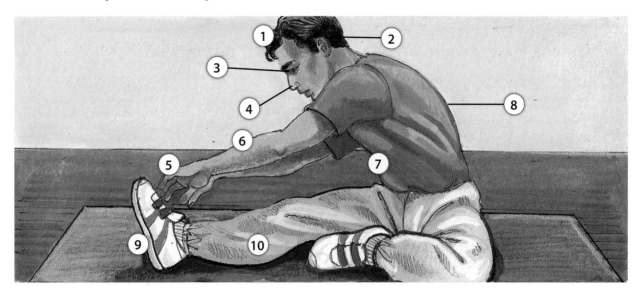

1. h e __a__ __d__
2. e a ____
3. e y ____
4. ____ ____ s e
5. h ____ n ____
6. a r ____
7. s ____ ____ m a c h
8. b ____ ____ k
9. ____ o o ____
10. ____ e g

B Copy the words from 2A in your notebook.

C Look at the pictures. Listen and follow the directions.

2-55

Point to your head.

Point to your leg.

D Work with a partner. Give directions. Listen and follow your partner's directions.

Point to your _____ .

▸▸ TEST YOURSELF

Use your notebook. Copy the chart. Write the words from the lesson in each column.

I have one	I have two
head	eyes

1 Learn about health problems

A Look at the picture. What parts of the body do you see?

B Listen and repeat the words.

2-56

1. a cold   4. a sore throat   7. a fever
2. a cough   5. a headache   8. the flu
3. an earache   6. a stomachache

C Look at the picture in 1A. Complete the sentences with the words from 1B.

1. Adam has an _earache_ .
2. Marge has a _____ .
3. Paula has a _____ .
4. Bella has a _____ and a _____ .
5. Harry has the _____ .
6. Thomas has a _____ _____ .

2 Prepare to write: email the doctor

A Listen and circle the appointment times you hear.
2-57

1. a. 12:00   2. a. 4:30   3. a. 3:00   4. a. 1:00
   b. 2:00   b. 5:30   b. 3:30   b. 10:00

B Listen again. Check (✓) the health problems you hear.
2-57

Daniela Lopez ①
name

☑ cough   ☐ earache

☐ fever   ☐ sore throat

☐ headache ☐ flu

☐ stomachache

Charlie Foss ②
name

☐ cough   ☐ earache

☐ fever   ☐ sore throat

☐ headache ☐ flu

☐ stomachache

Julie Chan ③
name

☐ cough   ☐ earache

☐ fever   ☐ sore throat

☐ headache ☐ flu

☐ stomachache

Colleen Rios ④
name

☐ cough   ☐ earache

☐ fever   ☐ sore throat

☐ headache ☐ flu

☐ stomachache

C Listen and read Paula's email.
2-58

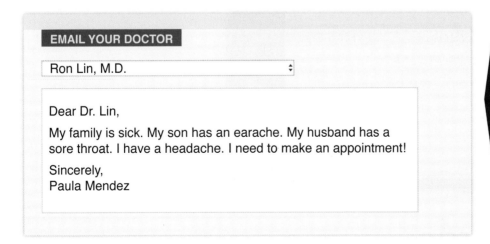

EMAIL YOUR DOCTOR

Ron Lin, M.D.

Dear Dr. Lin,

My family is sick. My son has an earache. My husband has a sore throat. I have a headache. I need to make an appointment!

Sincerely,
Paula Mendez

WRITER'S NOTE
In a note or an email:
Dear _____,
         (name)
...
...
...
Sincerely,

_____
(your name)

D Listen to Carl's story. Circle the correct word.

1. My daughter is _____ .   a. sick   b. sad
2. My son has a _____ .   a. headache   b. stomachache
3. I have a _____ .   a. cough   b. fever
4. I need to make an _____ .   a. earache   b. appointment

3 Write about health problems

Complete the sentences. Copy them in your notebook.

Dear Dr. Lin,

My _____ has _____ . I have _____ .

I need to make an _____ .

Sincerely,

_____

AT WORK ▶ Report sickness

A Look at the sickness report with your classmates. When is Allie's doctor appointment?

B Work with a partner. Look at the sickness report. Complete the sentences.

1. Allie's _____ is sick.

2. Her doctor appointment is in the _____ .

3. She is not going to work on _____ .

.ıll 🤶 ▣		12:34 PM
VACATION	**SICKNESS**	OTHER

Who Allie Thomas ▼👤   All day? ✓

Start 07/19/17 📅   End 07/19/17 📅

Notes My daughter is sick. I have a doctor appointment in the morning.

Report sickness

▶▶TEST YOURSELF

Look at the forms on page 105, 2B. Copy and complete the sentences.

Daniela has _____ . Charlie has _____ . Julie's _____ has _____ .

1 Use *have* and *has*

A Look at the pictures. Read the sentences.

He has a backache.

She has a toothache.

They have the flu.

B Study the form. Read the chart. Listen and repeat.

2-60

Have and *has*		
I You We They	have	the flu.
He She	has	

C Complete the sentences. Use *have* or *has*.

1. She _____ a backache.

2. We _____ the flu.

3. He _____ a toothache.

4. She _____ a stomachache.

D Look at the pictures. Complete the sentences. Use *has* or *have* and the health problem.

1. She _____ .

2. He _____ .

Use *have* and *has* to describe symptoms and ailments **107**

2 Practice: *yes/no* questions with *have*

A Look at the pictures. Listen to the questions and answers.

2-61

①

Dr. Tam: <u>Do you have</u> a sore throat?

Eva: <u>Yes, I do.</u>

Dr. Tam: <u>Do you have</u> a stomachache?

Eva: <u>No, I don't.</u>

②

Dr. Garcia: <u>Does he have</u> a fever?

Flor: <u>Yes, he does.</u>

Dr. Garcia: <u>Does he have</u> an earache?

Flor: <u>No, he doesn't.</u>

B Look at the picture. Complete the answers. Then complete the questions.

Leo   May   Zack   Terri

1. **A:** Does Leo have a headache?
   B: Yes, <u>he does</u> .

2. **A:** Does Terri have a stomachache?
   B: No, _____ .

3. **A:** Does May have a cough?
   B: Yes, _____ .

4. **A:** Do they have toothaches?
   B: No, _____ .

5. **A:** <u>Does</u> Terri <u>have</u> a backache?
   B: No, she doesn't.

6. **A:** _____ Zack _____ a fever?
   B: Yes, he does.

7. **A:** _____ May _____ a sore throat?
   B: Yes, she does.

8. **A:** _____ Leo _____ a stomachache?
   B: Yes, he does.

C Talk to three classmates. Ask and answer the question.

A: *Do you have _____ ?*

B: *Yes, I do. / No, I don't.*

3 Ask and answer questions about health problems

A Look at the pictures. Listen and repeat the conversations.

2-62

1. **A:** Does she have the flu?
   B: Yes, she does.

2. **A:** Does he have a stomachache?
   B: No, he doesn't. He has a cold.

B Work with a partner. Practice the conversations. Talk about the pictures.

Mack   Rita   Timmy

Bob   Ken   May

A: Does Bob have a stomachache?
B: Yes, he does.
A: Does Bob have a fever?
B: No, he doesn't. He has a stomachache.

▶▶ TEST YOURSELF

Write sentences about three of the pictures in Exercise 3.

Bob has a stomachache. Timmy has an earache.

1 Listen for medical appointment information

🔊 **A** Listen to the phone calls. Point to the days you hear.
2-63

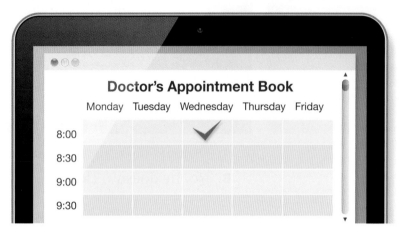

Doctor's Appointment Book

	Monday	Tuesday	Wednesday	Thursday	Friday
8:00			✓		
8:30					
9:00					
9:30					

🔊 **B** Listen again. Check (✓) the day and time in the calendar.
2-63

C Work with a partner. Point to the calendar. Ask and answer the question.

A: When is the appointment?

B: It's on Wednesday at 8:00.

2 Practice your pronunciation

🔊 **A** Listen for the different sounds of *a*.
2-64

matter	*ache*
1. have	7. say
2. has	8. name
3. sad	9. plane
4. hand	10.
5.	11.
6.	12.

🔊 **B** Listen and write these words in the chart.
2-65

| ~~hand~~ | happy | back | grapes | day | make |

🔊 **C** Listen again and check your answers.
2-65

3 Make conversation: make a doctor's appointment

A Look at the pictures. Read the conversation.

 B Listen and read.

2-66

Receptionist:	Hello, Downtown Clinic.	**Kara:**	I have a stomachache.
Kara:	This is Kara Woods.	**Receptionist:**	Is 2:00 OK?
	I need to see the doctor.	**Kara:**	Yes, thank you.
Receptionist:	What's the matter?		

 C Listen again and repeat.

2-66

D Work with a partner. Make a new conversation. Use your own ideas.

A: Hello. Downtown Clinic.

B: This is _____ . I need to see the doctor.

A: What's the matter?

B: I have a _____ .

A: Is _____ OK?

B: Yes, thank you.

NEED HELP?

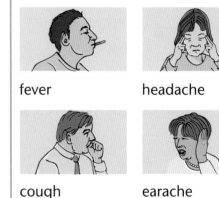

fever   headache

cough   earache

▶▶ **TEST YOURSELF**

Practice with a partner. Then switch roles.

Student A: Look at the conversation in 3D. You are the receptionist.
Student B: Close your book. You need to see the doctor.

1 Get ready to read

A Look at the calendars. Listen and repeat.

2-67

1

SUNDAY ✓	WEDNESDAY ✓	SATURDAY ✓
MONDAY ✓	THURSDAY ✓	
TUESDAY ✓	FRIDAY ✓	

every day

2

SUNDAY ✓✓	WEDNESDAY ✓✓	SATURDAY ✓✓
MONDAY ✓✓	THURSDAY ✓✓	
TUESDAY ✓✓	FRIDAY ✓✓	

twice a day

3

SUNDAY ✓✓✓	WEDNESDAY ✓✓✓	SATURDAY ✓✓✓
MONDAY ✓✓✓	THURSDAY ✓✓✓	
TUESDAY ✓✓✓	FRIDAY ✓✓✓	

three times a day

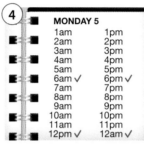

4

MONDAY 5

1am	1pm
2am	2pm
3am	3pm
4am	4pm
5am	5pm
6am ✓	6pm ✓
7am	7pm
8am	8pm
9am	9pm
10am	10pm
11am	11pm
12pm ✓	12am ✓

every six hours

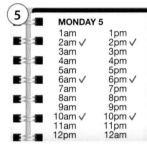

5

MONDAY 5

1am	1pm
2am ✓	2pm ✓
3am	3pm
4am	4pm
5am	5pm
6am ✓	6pm ✓
7am	7pm
8am	8pm
9am	9pm
10am ✓	10pm ✓
11am	11pm
12pm	12am

every four hours

B Match the frequency with the times.

_____ 1. every four hours
_____ 2. every day
_____ 3. every six hours
_____ 4. twice a day
_____ 5. three times a day

a. 8 a.m., 8 p.m.
b. 8 a.m., 2 p.m., 8 p.m., 2 a.m.
c. 8 a.m., 12 p.m., 4, p.m., 8 p.m., 12 a.m., 4 a.m.
d. 8 a.m., 4 p.m., 12 a.m.
e. Sun., Mon., Tues., Wed., Thurs., Fri., Sat.

C Look at the pictures. Read the words/sentences.

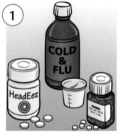

1

medicine

2

CoughX
Take 1 teaspoon
twice a day.

label

3

tsp

teaspoon

4

tbsp

tablespoon

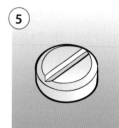

5

tablet

D What medicine do you have at home? Check (✓) the boxes.

☐ I have headache medicine.

☐ I have earache medicine.

☐ I have cough medicine.

☐ I have cold medicine.

2 Read medicine labels

A Read the medicine labels. What are the medicines for?

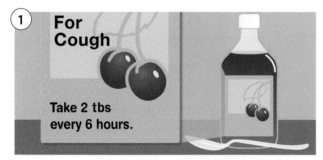

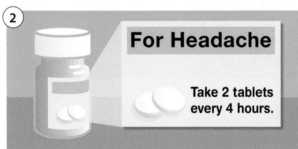

B Look at the medicine labels. Circle *a* or *b*.

1. Medicine 1: _____ .
   a. take six tablespoons   b. take two tablespoons

2. Medicine 2: _____ .
   a. take every two hours   b. take every four hours

3. Medicine 3: _____ .
   a. take three times a day   b. take two times a day

4. Medicine 4: _____ .
   a. take for a cough   b. take for a cold

5. Medicine 4: _____ .
   a. take one tablespoon   b. take one teaspoon

> **READING NOTE**
> tsp. = teaspoon
> tbs. = tablespoon

 BRING IT TO LIFE

Bring in medicine from the store or from a doctor.
Circle one new word.

TEAMWORK & LANGUAGE REVIEW

A Work with a team. Talk about the picture. Say what you see.

Lucas

B Write the words you know in the chart.

Parts of the body	Health problems	Other

C Look up three words you don't know in a dictionary.
Add them to the chart.

D Look at the picture in A. Complete the sentences. Use the words in the box.

tablespoon	appointment	~~sick~~	work
has	doctor	medicine	

1. Lucas is ____sick____ .
2. He _____ a fever.
3. His cough _____ is on the table.
4. He takes one _____ every four hours.
5. He isn't going to _____ today.
6. He needs to see the _____ .
7. He has an _____ at 10 a.m.

PROBLEM SOLVING

2-68

A Listen. Look at the pictures.

Orane's Problem

B Work with your classmates. Help Orane.

a. Go to work.   b. Go to the doctor.   c. Stay home.

UNIT

9 What Size?

A LOOK AT
- Colors and clothes
- The present continuous
- Dress codes

LESSON 1 VOCABULARY

1 Learn colors

A Look at the picture. Count the shoes.

B Listen and point to the colors.
3-02

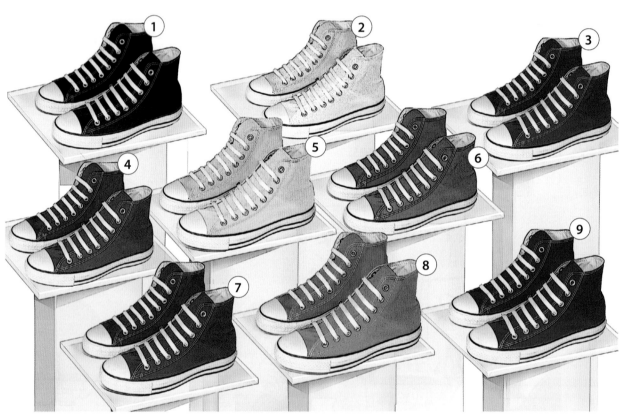

C Listen and repeat the words.
3-02

1. black	4. blue	7. brown
2. white	5. yellow	8. orange
3. red	6. green	9. purple

D Say the new words with a partner.

E Work with a partner. Cover the words. Point to the picture. Say the words.

2 Talk about colors

A Look at the picture. Complete the words.

1. r __e__ d
2. g r ___ e ___
3. ___ h i ___ e

4. b ___ ___ c k
5. ___ r ___ w ___
6. ___ r ___ n g ___

7. y ___ l ___ o w
8. ___ l ___ e
9. ___ u ___ p l e

B Copy the words from 2A in your notebook.

3-03 **C Listen and repeat.**

    A: What color is this sweater?

    B: It's red.

    A: What color is this shirt?

    B: It's purple.

D Work with a partner. Point to the clothes in 2A. Practice the conversations.

    A: What color is this ____ ?

    B: It's ____ .

E Talk to three classmates. Ask and answer the question.

    A: What is your favorite color?

    B: My favorite color is _____ .

▶▶TEST YOURSELF

Close your book. Write five colors. Check your spelling.

1 Learn about clothes

A Look at the pictures. What clothes do you see?

July

October

February

B Listen and repeat the words.

3-04

1. hat   5. dress
2. T-shirt   6. coat
3. shorts   7. belt
4. jacket   8. boots

C Look at the pictures in 1A. Complete the sentences.

1. It's July. Justine is wearing white ___shorts___ , a red _____ ,
   and a blue _____ .

2. It's October. She's wearing a blue and white _____ and a purple
   _____ .

3. It's February. She's wearing a yellow _____ , a white _____ ,
   and brown _____ .

2 Prepare to write: my clothes

A Listen for clothes and colors. Circle *a* or *b*.

3-05

1. a.   b.

2. a.   b.

3. a.   b.

4. a.   b.

B Work with a partner. Talk about the pictures in 1A and 2A.

It's a red dress. It's a red sweater.

C Look at the pictures. Listen and read the sentences.

3-06

It's hot.   It's warm.   It's cool.   It's cold.

D Check (✓) the weather you like.

☐ hot   ☐ warm   ☐ cool   ☐ cold

E Listen and read Justine's story.

3-07

> It's July. It's hot today. I'm wearing a red T-shirt, white shorts, and a blue hat.

WRITER'S NOTE

Use commas [,] in a list of three:

I'm wearing
<u>a blue shirt</u>,
<u>black pants</u>, and
<u>brown shoes</u>.

F Listen to Ben's story. Circle the correct word.

1. It's _____ . (a.) January   b. June
2. It's _____ today.   a. cold   b. warm
3. I'm wearing a blue _____   a. coat   b. belt
   and a brown _____ .   a. belt   b. boot

Ben

3 Write about your clothes

A Write the month. Write about your clothes today. Complete the sentences.

It's _____ .

It's _____ today.

I'm wearing _____ , _____ , and _____ .

B Read your story to a partner.

AT WORK ▶ **Dress codes**

A Read the memo.

Dress Code for Salespeople

- a white shirt and black pants
- black shoes
- a black jacket

Don't wear:
- T-shirts
- shorts
- hats
- sweaters

☐ Kevin

☐ John

B Look at the salespeople. Who is following the dress code?
Check (✓) the picture.

▶▶ **TEST YOURSELF**

Write what one of your classmates is wearing.

Maria is wearing a jacket.

_____ is wearing _____ .

1 Use statements with the present continuous

A Listen and read the sentences.

3-09

1

I'm wearing black pants.

2

She's wearing a blue dress.

3

They're wearing shorts.

B Study the form. Read the charts. Listen and repeat.

3-10

The Present Continuous		
Affirmative Statements		
I	am	
You	are	
He She It	is	wearing shoes.
We They	are	

NEED HELP?

Contractions
You can use contractions
with the present continuous.
I'm wearing shoes.
You**'re wearing** shoes.
He**'s wearing** shoes.
They**'re wearing** shoes.

C Complete the sentences. Circle *a* or *b*.

1. I ____ shoes.
   a. is wearing   (b.) am wearing
2. You are ____ shoes.
   a. wear   b. wearing

3. He is ____ black pants.
   a. wearing   b. wears
4. They ____ red hats.
   a. wearing   b. are wearing

D Work with a partner. Talk about what people in the class are wearing.
Use contractions.

I'm wearing _____ .
She's wearing _____ .
He's wearing _____ .

2 Practice: *yes/no* questions with the present continuous

A Look at the pictures. Listen and read the questions and answers.

3-11

A: <u>Are you wearing a dress?</u>
B: Yes, I am.

A: <u>Is Ed reading a book?</u>
B: Yes, he is.

A: <u>Is Min reading a book?</u>
B: No, she's not.

A: <u>Is the cat sleeping?</u>
B: Yes, it is.

A: <u>Are we going to the party?</u>
B: No, we're not.

A: <u>Are they wearing red shoes?</u>
B: No, they're not.

B Complete the questions. Use the present continuous.

1. **A:** _____ Kip sleeping?
   B: No, he's not.

2. **A:** _____ Irene wearing a purple sweater?
   B: No, she's not.

3. **A:** _____ Irene and Malia walking?
   B: Yes, they are.

4. **A:** Is Malia _____ a book?
   B: No, she's not.

5. **A:** Are Fred and Nancy _____ shorts?
   B: No, they aren't.

6. **A:** Is Kip _____ shorts?
   B: Yes, he is.

Kip

Irene   Malia

Nancy   Fred

C Work with a partner. Read the questions and answers in 2A and 2B. Ask more questions about the pictures in 2B.

Is _____ wearing _____ ?

3 Ask and answer questions about clothing

A Look at the pictures. Listen and repeat.

3-12

1. **A:** Is he wearing a yellow hat?

   B: Yes, he is.

2. **A:** Is she wearing black pants?

   B: No, she's not. She's wearing a dress.

B Work with a partner. Practice the conversations.
Talk about the pictures in 3A.

1. **A:** Is he wearing a yellow hat?

   B: Yes, he is.

2. **A:** Is she wearing red pants?

   B: No, she's not. She's wearing a dress.

C Work with two classmates. Follow the directions. Take turns.

Close your eyes. Think about what your classmates are wearing.
Ask questions.

Is Marta wearing a blue sweater?

▶▶ TEST YOURSELF

Work with a partner. Write questions and answers about three of the pictures in 3A.
Take turns.

Is he wearing a green hat?

No, he's not.

1 Listen for sizes and prices

A Look at the picture. What color are the T-shirts? Are they on sale?

B Listen. Circle *a* or *b*.

3-13

1. a. large   b. extra-large   3. a. large   b. medium
2. a. small   b. medium   4. a. small   b. extra-large

C Listen. Write the prices on the receipt.

3-14

D Do the math. Write the total on the receipt.

The Clothes Spot	
dress	$_____._____
jacket	$_____._____
sub-total	$_____._____
tax 5%	$_____._____
Total	$_____._____

2 Practice your pronunciation

A Listen for the contraction *I'm*.

3-15

I'm	I
I'm looking	I look
I'm wearing	I wear

B Listen. Circle the form you hear.

3-16

1. I   I'm   4. I   I'm
2. I   I'm   5. I   I'm
3. I   I'm   6. I   I'm

C Listen again and repeat.

3-16

3 Make conversation: shopping for clothes

A Look at the pictures. Read the conversation.

B Listen and read.

3-17

Hector: Excuse me. I'm looking for an orange T-shirt.

Clerk: What size?

Hector: Small.

Clerk: Here's a small. It's $12.

Hector: Thanks.

C Listen again and repeat.

3-17

D Work with a partner. Make a new conversation. Use your own ideas.

A: I'm looking for _____ .

B: What size?

A: _____ .

B: Here's _____ . It's _____ .

A: Thanks.

NEED HELP?

I'm looking for...

a T-shirt	a jacket
a shirt	a belt
a coat	a dress

▶▶ **TEST YOURSELF**

Work with a partner. Student A, look at the conversation in 3D.
Student B, close your book. Practice the conversation.
Then switch roles.

1 Get ready to read

A Look at the pictures. Listen and repeat.
3-18

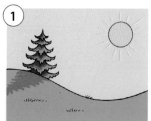
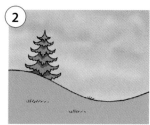
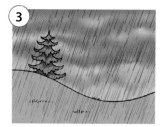

It's sunny.   It's cloudy.   It's raining.   It's snowing.

B Look at the pictures. Complete the sentences.

1.   It's _____ . He's wearing shorts.

2.   It's _____ . She's reading a book.

3.   It's _____ . They're playing soccer.

4.   It's _____ . He's sleeping.

C Read the weather website.

D Check (✓) the weather in your city today.

☐ hot   ☐ cool   ☐ sunny   ☐ raining

☐ warm   ☐ cold   ☐ cloudy   ☐ snowing

2 Read about weather in Seattle, Washington

A Read the paragraph and the bar graph.

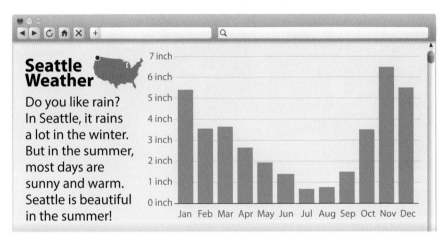

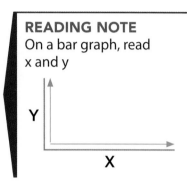

READING NOTE
On a bar graph, read x and y

B Listen and read the sentences again.

3-19

C Look at the sentences and the bar graph. Circle the correct word.

1. In Seattle, it rains a lot in _____ .   May   December

2. It rains about 5 inches in _____ .   July   January

3. It rains about 1.5 inches in _____ .   September   October

4. It rains about 4 inches in _____ .   April   February

5. It's sunny and warm in the _____ .   spring   summer

BRING IT TO LIFE

Look up your city's weather online.
Copy one new word.

A Work with a team. Talk about the picture. Say what you see.

B Write the words you know in the chart.

Colors	Clothes	Other

C Look up three words you don't know in a dictionary. Add them to the chart.

D **Look at the picture in A. Write the answers and complete the questions.**

1. **A:** Is Al wearing a white shirt?

   B: ___Yes, he is___ .

2. **A:** Is Bob wearing shorts?

   B: _____ .

3. **A:** Is Mona wearing a yellow T-shirt?

   B: _____ .

4. **A:** _____ a green dress?

   B: Yes, she is.

5. **A:** _____ black pants?

   B: No, he isn't.

6. **A:** _____ a dress?

   B: No, she isn't.

E **Write two more questions and answers.**

Is _____ wearing _____ ?

_____

PROBLEM SOLVING

A **Listen. Look at the pictures.**

3-20

Ethan's Problem

B **Work with your classmates. Help Ethan.**

a. Wear it.

b. Put it in the closet.

c. Return it.

d. Other: _____

UNIT

10 This Is My Home

A LOOK AT
- The home
- Possessives and prepositions
- Asking about a rental

LESSON 1 VOCABULARY

1 Learn about rooms and things in the home

A Look at the pictures. Say the words you know.

B Listen and point to the pictures.
3-21

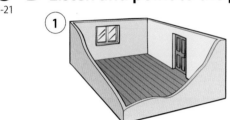  

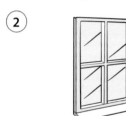  

C Listen and repeat the words.
3-21

1. room	4. sofa	7. TV
2. window	5. bed	8. stove
3. furniture	6. dresser	9. refrigerator

D Say the new words with a partner.

E Work with a partner. Cover the words. Point to the picture. Say the words.

2 Talk about a home

A **Look at the pictures. Complete the words.**

kitchen   bedroom   living room

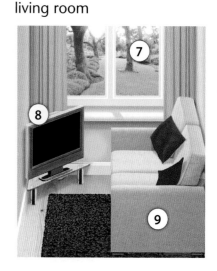

1. ___ o o ___
2. r e f ___ ___ g e r a t ___ ___
3. ___ t o ___ e
4. d r ___ s ___ e r
5. ___ ___ d

6. f u r ___ i ___ ___ r e
7. w ___ n ___ ___ w
8. ___ ___
9. s ___ ___ ___

B **Copy the words from 2A in your notebook.**

3-22

C **Listen and repeat.**

1. **A:** Where's the stove?
   B: It's in the kitchen.

2. **A:** Where's the sofa?
   B: It's in the living room.

3. **A:** Where's the dresser?
   B: It's in the bedroom.

4. **A:** Where's the refrigerator?
   B: It's in the kitchen.

D **Work with a partner. Point to the pictures in 2A.**
Practice the conversation.

A: Where's the _____ ?
B: It's in the _____ .

▸▸**TEST YOURSELF**

Use your notebook. Copy this chart.
Write words from the lesson in each column.

furniture	rooms	other

1 Learn about an apartment building

A Look at the picture. How many windows are in the apartment?

B Listen and repeat the words.

3-23

1. apartment building
2. apartment
3. first floor
4. second floor

5. stairs
6. bathroom
7. garage
8. door

C Look at the picture in 1A. Complete the sentences.

1. The _apartment building_ has two floors.
2. Peter's apartment is on the _____ .
3. Apartment A is on the _____ .
4. The _____ are gray.
5. The _____ is green.
6. Peter's _____ is blue.
7. Peter's _____ has a small kitchen.
8. A car is in the _____ .

2 Prepare to write: my home

A Listen and point to the rooms.

3-24

Jill's Apartment

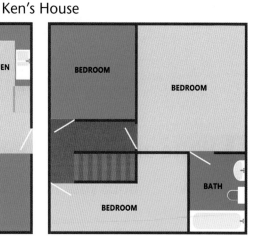

Ken's House

First Floor

Second Floor

B Look at the house and the apartment. Complete the sentences with the words in the box.

small	~~living room~~	floor	bedrooms	large	bathroom

1. Jill's apartment has one __living room__ .
2. Her kitchen is very _____ .
3. Ken lives in a _____ house.
4. His bedroom is on the second _____ .
5. The house has three _____ .
6. The _____ is on the first floor.

C Listen and read Peter's story.

3-25

> ### My Apartment
>
> My apartment is small. It's on the second floor next to the stairs. It has one bedroom and one bathroom. It has a small kitchen. I like my apartment.

WRITER'S NOTE
The title of this story is *My Apartment*. Give your story a title.

D Listen to Meg's story. Circle the correct word.

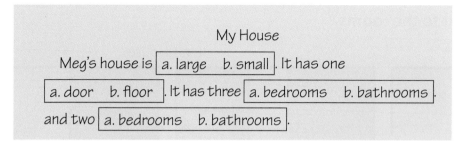

My House

Meg's house is | a. large   b. small |. It has one
| a. door   b. floor |. It has three | a. bedrooms   b. bathrooms |.
and two | a. bedrooms   b. bathrooms |.

Meg

3 Write about your home

A Write about your home. Complete the sentences.

_____
title

My home is _____ . It has _____ .

It has _____

B Read your story to a partner.

AT WORK **Safety**

A Look at the pictures. Listen to the woman talk about safety at work.

The smoke alarm is on the ceiling.

The fire extinguisher is on the wall.

The caution sign is on the floor.

B Work with a partner. Read the sentences in A. Then talk about the pictures.

_Do you have a ____ at work? Do you have a ____ at home? Where is it?_

▶ TEST YOURSELF

Write two sentences about the apartment and the house in 2A.

The house has _____ . The apartment has _____ .

1 Explore possessive 's

A Look at the pictures. Listen and read the sentences.

3-28

Teng's house is white.

Gloria's house is small.

Mr. and Mrs. Smith's home is big.

Karen's bedroom is green.

B Match the sentences.

_c_ 1. His house is white.

____ 2. Her home is small.

____ 3. Their home is big.

____ 4. Her bedroom is green.

____ 5. His living room is big.

a. Lionel's living room is big.

b. Karen's bedroom is green.

c. Teng's house is white.

d. Mr. and Mrs. Smith's home is big.

e. Gloria's home is small.

C Look at the pictures. Complete the sentences. Write about the pictures.

Min

Alba

Taylor

Mr. and Mrs. Brown

1. _____Taylor's_____ living room is black and white.

2. _____ TV is in the kitchen.

3. _____ kitchen is small.

4. _____ sofa is purple.

D Work with a partner. Talk about people you know.

My sister's kitchen is big. Alan's house is small. Peter's kitchen is small.

2 Learn about prepositions of location

3-29

A Look at the pictures. Listen and read the sentences.

The shirt is **on** the dresser.

The shirt is **in** the dresser.

The stove is **next to** the sink.

The stove is **between** the refrigerator and the sink.

The window is **over** the sofa.

The sofa is **under** the window.

B Look at the picture. Complete the sentences. Circle *a* or *b*.

1. The book is ____ the picture.
   a. next to   b. between
2. The window is ____ the bed.
   a. over   b. under
3. The pants are ____ the bed.
   a. in   b. on
4. The clock is ____ the wall.
   a. in   b. on

5. The bed is ____ the window.
   a. over   b. under
6. The socks are ____ the dresser.
   a. in   b. on
7. The table is ____ the dresser.
   a. next to   b. on
8. The table is ____ the window and the dresser.
   a. over   b. between

3 Ask about locations

A Look at the pictures. Complete the sentences.

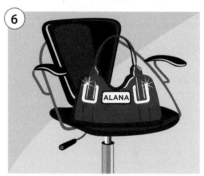

1. ___Mario's___ computer is on the floor.
2. _____ books are under the desk.
3. _____ apple is next to the computer.
4. _____ jacket is on the stairs.
5. _____ pencils are in the bathroom.
6. _____ purse is on the chair.

B Read the conversations. Listen and repeat.

3-30

1. **A:** Where's Mario's <u>computer</u>?

   B: It's on the floor.

2. **A:** Where are Jill's <u>books</u>?

   B: They're under the <u>desk</u>.

C Work with a partner. Ask and answer questions about the pictures in 3A.

A: *Where's Ben's _____ ?*   **A:** *Where are Beth's _____ ?*

B: *It's _____ .*   **B:** *They're _____ .*

▸▸ TEST YOURSELF

Write three sentences about things in your classroom.

Kay's pencils are on the table.   The teacher's desk is next to the window.

1 Listen for large numbers

🔊 **A** **Listen to the numbers. Repeat.**
3-31

200	1,000	3,500	100,000
450	2,250	10,000	250,000

🔊 **B** **Listen. Check (✓) the number you hear.**
3-32

1. 2,500 ____ 250 ✓   4. 3,100 ____ 301 ____
2. 60,000 ____ 6,000 ____   5. 180,000 ____ 18,000 ____
3. 1,250 ____ 125,000 ____   6. 1,250 ____ 1,520 ____

🔊 **C** **Listen. Write the numbers. Then do the math.**
3-33

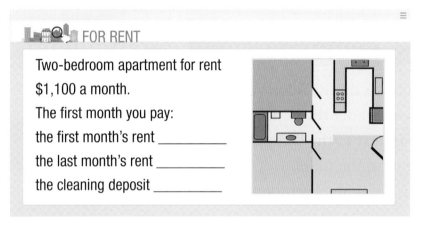

FOR RENT

Two-bedroom apartment for rent
$1,100 a month.
The first month you pay:
the first month's rent _____
the last month's rent _____
the cleaning deposit _____

$ __1,100__ + $ _____ + $ _____ = $ _____
  first month's rent   last month's rent   cleaning deposit   deposit

How much do you pay in the first month for this apartment? _____

2 Practice your pronunciation

🔊 **A** **Listen for the stressed syllable.**
3-34

1st syllable	Last syllable	Middle syllable
bedroom	ga**rage**	a**part**ment
thirty	thir**teen**	com**pu**ter

🔊 **B** **Listen and** underline **the stressed syllable.**
3-35

1. <u>bath</u>room   3. alarm   5. furniture
2. fourteen   4. November   6. sofa

🔊 **C** **Listen again and check your answers. Repeat the words.**
3-35

3 Make conversation: ask about a home for rent

A Look at the pictures. Read the conversation.

B Listen and read.
3-36

Diana: Is there an apartment for rent?

Manager: Yes, there is.

Diana: How much is the rent?

Manager: The rent is $900. The deposit is $600.

C Listen again and repeat.
3-36

D Work with a partner. Make a new conversation. Use your own ideas.

A: Is there _____ for rent?

B: Yes, there is.

A: How much is the rent?

B: It's _____ .

> **NEED HELP?**
>
> Is there _____ for rent?
> a house
> a room
> an apartment

▶▶ TEST YOURSELF

Work with a partner. Student A, look at the conversation in 3D.
Student B, close your book. Practice the conversation. Then switch roles.

1 Get ready to read

A Look at the pictures. Listen and repeat.

3-37

condo

townhouse

mobile home

B Listen. Circle *a* or *b*.

3-38

1. a. condo   b. apartment
2. a. townhouse   b. mobile home
3. a. house   b. mobile home
4. a. condo   b. townhouse
5. a. house   b. apartment

C Look at the pictures. Read the abbreviations and the words.

apt = apartment

BR = bedroom

BA = bathroom

D Complete the sentence. Do you live in a *house, apartment, condo, townhouse,* or *mobile home*?

I live in a _____ .

2 Read housing ads

READING NOTE
a month = every month

A Read the housing ads.

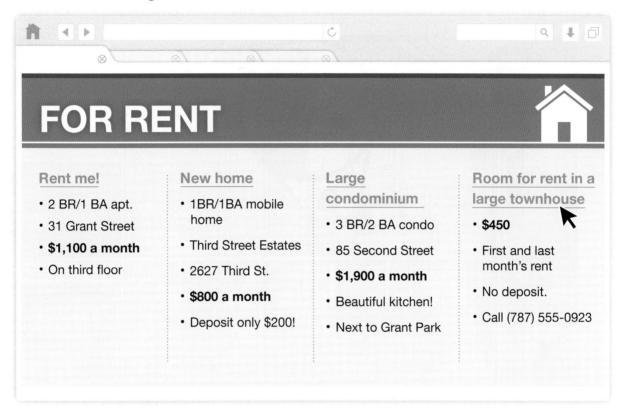

FOR RENT

Rent me!
- 2 BR/1 BA apt.
- 31 Grant Street
- **$1,100 a month**
- On third floor

New home
- 1BR/1BA mobile home
- Third Street Estates
- 2627 Third St.
- **$800 a month**
- Deposit only $200!

Large condominium
- 3 BR/2 BA condo
- 85 Second Street
- **$1,900 a month**
- Beautiful kitchen!
- Next to Grant Park

Room for rent in a large townhouse
- **$450**
- First and last month's rent
- No deposit.
- Call (787) 555-0923

B Look at the housing ads. Circle *True* or *False*.

1. The apartment is on Grant Street.	(True)	False
2. The apartment has two bedrooms.	True	False
3. The condominium has two bathrooms.	True	False
4. The mobile home rent is $1,100 a month.	True	False
5. The room for rent is $800 a month.	True	False
6. The condominium is on Third Street.	True	False

 BRING IT TO LIFE

Find a housing ad online.

Copy two abbreviations.

TEAMWORK & LANGUAGE REVIEW

A Work with a team. Talk about the picture. Say what you see.

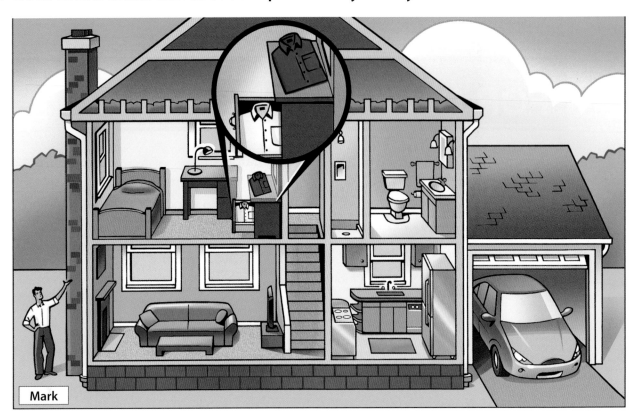

Mark

B Write the words you know in the chart.

Parts of the house	Furniture	Other
window	bed	refrigerator

C Look up three words you don't know in a dictionary. Add them to the chart.

D **Look at the picture of Mark's house. Complete the sentences with *in*, *on*, *next to*, *between*, *over*, or *under*.**

1. Mark's blue shirt is _____on_____ the dresser.

2. His white shirt is _____ the dresser.

3. His desk is _____ the window.

4. His lamp is _____ the desk.

5. The garage is _____ the kitchen.

6. The stairs are _____ the kitchen and the living room.

7. The TV is _____ the living room.

8. In the kitchen, the window is _____ the sink.

PROBLEM SOLVING

A **Listen. Look at the pictures.**

3-39

Mr. and Mrs. Kolda's Problem

B **Work with your classmates. Help Mr. and Mrs. Kolda.**

a. Light candles.

b. Call the electric company.

c. Call 911.

d. Other: _____

UNIT

11 Where's the Bank?

A LOOK AT
- Community
- Present continuous questions
- Work activities

LESSON 1 VOCABULARY

1 Learn places in the community

A Look at the pictures. Say what you see.

B Listen and point to the pictures.

3-40

C Listen and repeat the words.

3-40

1. bookstore
2. bus station
3. drugstore
4. bank
5. restaurant
6. supermarket
7. gym
8. bakery
9. gas station

D Say the new words with a partner.

E Work with a partner. Cover the words. Point to the pictures. Say the words.

2 Talk about places in the community

A Look at the pictures. Complete the words.

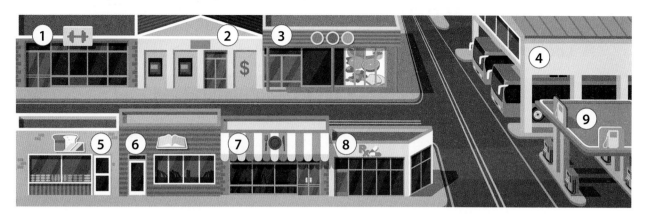

1. g _y_ _m_
2. b ___ n ___
3. s ___ p e r m ___ r k ___ t
4. b ___ s s t a ___ i o ___
5. ___ a k e ___ ___

6. b ___ o k s ___ o ___ e
7. r e s ___ ___ u r a n ___
8. ___ r ___ g s t o ___ e
9. ___ a s s ___ a t i ___ n

B Copy the words from 2A in your notebook.

C Listen and repeat.

3-41

1. **A:** Where is he?

   B: He's at the bus station.

2. **A:** Where are they?

   B: They're at the park.

D Work with a partner. Point to the picture in 2A. Practice the conversation.

1. **A:** Where is he?

   B: He's at the bank.

2. **A:** Where is she?

   B: She's at the bank.

3. **A:** Where are they?

   B: They're at the restaurant.

E Talk to three classmates. Ask and answer the question.

A: Where do you go every week?

B: I go to the supermarket every week.

▶▶ TEST YOURSELF

Close your book. Write four places in the community. Check your spelling.

1 Learn about activities

A Look at the pictures. Where are the people?

B Listen and repeat the words.

3-42

1 play   3. exercise   5. wash   7. drink

2. walk   4. buy   6. eat   8. use

C Complete the sentences with the words from 1B. Use the words in the box.

washing	~~walking~~	drinking	using
playing	buying	eating	exercising

1. A man and woman are ___walking___ in the park.

2. Two women are _____ lunch at the restaurant.

3. A woman is _____ in the park.

4. A man is _____ coffee at the restaurant.

5. Pia is _____ her clothes.

6. A man is _____ the ATM.

7. A man is _____ gas.

8. The children are _____ .

2 Prepare to write

Listen for places and actions. Number the pictures.

3-43

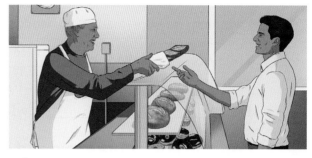

____

1

____

____

B Look at the pictures in 2A. Complete the sentences.

1. My brother is at the _____ .
   He's buying bread.

2. My parents are drinking tea.
   They're at a _____ .

3. My friends are at the _____ . They're _____ lunch.

4. My sister is at the _____ . She's _____ .

> **NEED HELP?**
>
> Look at the words in 1C on page 146.

C Listen again and check your answers.

3-43

D Listen and read Pia's paragraph.

3-44

> **My Saturday**
> Today is Saturday. My husband is at the gas station. He's buying gas. I'm at the laudromat. I'm washing my clothes.

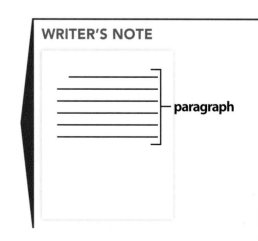

WRITER'S NOTE

paragraph

Unit 11 Lesson 2 **147**

E Listen to Rob's paragraph. Where is his wife?

3-45

F Complete the sentences. Use the words in the box.

washing	supermarket	work	buying	~~Wednesday~~

Today is _____Wednesday_____ . Rob's wife is at the _____ .

She's _____ food. His brother is at _____ .

He's _____ windows.

G Listen to Rob's story again and check your answers.

3-45

3 Write

A Think about your friends and family. Where are they? What are they doing? Write a title. Complete the paragraph.

_____

Today is _____ . My _____

is at _____ . He's _____ .

My _____ is at _____ .

She's _____ .

B Read your story to a partner.

AT WORK ▶ **Job duties**

Listen. Read the words. What things do you use at work?

3-46

Jim

making copies
using a photocopier

Ben

cleaning the floor
using a mop

Thea

helping customers
using a cash register

▶▶ TEST YOURSELF

Draw or show a picture of yourself. Write two sentences about the picture.

I'm at _____ . I'm _____ .

1 Explore present continuous verbs

A Listen and read the sentences.

3-47

① She's listening to music. ② He's drinking water. ③ They're talking.

B Listen and repeat the verbs. Study the spelling.

3-48

verb	+*ing*	verb	+*ing*
buy	buying	exercise	exercising
call	calling	make	making
drink	drinking	use	using
eat	eating	write	writing
listen	listening		
play	playing		
talk	talking		
walk	walking		
wash	washing		
work	working		

C Work with a partner. Spell the verbs in the chart. Take turns.

buy

buying
B-U-Y-I-N-G

D Work with a partner. Use the chart to make sentences.

I	am	eating	lunch.
He	is	drinking	coffee.
She	are	buying	bread.
They		calling	my friend.

2 Practice: present continuous questions and answers

A Read the questions and answers.

A: What are you doing?

B: I'm cleaning the tables.

A: What is she doing?

B: She's cooking.

A: What are they doing?

B: They're washing the dishes.

B Look at the pictures. Complete the questions. Circle *a* or *b*.

1. What _____ doing?
   a. he is
   b. is he

3. What _____ doing?
   a. is she
   b. she is

2. What _____ doing?
   a. they are
   b. are they

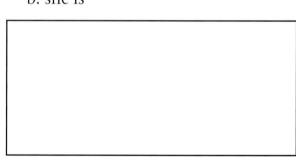

4. What _____ doing?
   a. are you
   b. you are

C Work with a partner. Ask and answer the questions in 2B. Use the answers below.

She's writing.

He's eating lunch.

They're walking.

I'm _____ .

3 Ask and answer questions with *What* and *Where*

A Look at the picture. Listen and read the conversations.

A: Where are they?
B: They're at the office.
A: What is Tom doing?
B: He's reading.

A: What is Jill doing?
B: She's using a computer.
A: What are Rick and Steve doing?
B: They're talking.

B Look at the pictures. Complete the questions and answers.

1. A: Where _____ ?
   B: _____ at work.
   A: What _____ doing?
   B: _____ a computer.

2. A: Where _____ ?
   B: _____ at school.
   A: What _____ doing?
   B: _____ .

C Work with a partner. Read the questions and answers in 3B. Then ask and answer questions about the people in 3A. Use *Where* and *What*.

▶▶ TEST YOURSELF

Write two questions and two answers about a picture on page 144.

Where _____ ?   What _____ ?

_____   _____

1 Listen for locations

🔊 **A** Listen for the locations. Point to the places.
3-50

B Work with a partner. Ask and answer the questions. Use the answers in the box.

1. Where is the supermarket?
2. Where are the schools?
3. Where is the bookstore?

> They're on Ash Street.
> It's on Oak Street.
> It's next to the restaurant.
> It's between the post office and the clothing store.

2 Practice your pronunciation

🔊 **A** Listen for the *th* sounds.
3-51

there	thank
the	thirsty
then	Thursday

_____   _____

_____

🔊 **B** Listen to these words. Then write them in the correct place
3-52 in the chart in 2A.

three   these   they

C Listen again. Repeat the words.

3 Make conversation: talk about locations

A Look at the pictures. Read the conversation.

Excuse me. I'm looking for the drugstore.

It's over there, next to the bookstore.

Mario   Phu

Thank you.

You're welcome.

🔊
3-54

B Listen and read.

Mario: Excuse me. I'm looking for the drugstore.

Phu: It's over there, next to the bookstore.

Mario: Thank you.

Phu: You're welcome.

🔊
3-54

C Listen again and repeat.

D Work with a partner. Make a new conversation. Use the picture in 3A.

A: Excuse me. I'm looking for the _____ .

B: It's _____ .

A: Thanks.

B: You're welcome.

▶▶**TEST YOURSELF**

Work with a partner. Practice the conversation in 3D. Ask about a place in your community.

1 Get ready to read

 A Look at the pictures. Listen and repeat.

3-55

Department of Motor
Vehicles (DMV)

fire station

ambulance

police station

hospital

courthouse

B Listen. Circle *a* or *b*.

3-56

1. a.  b.

2. a.  b.

3. a.  b.

4. a.  b.

C Look at the pictures. Read the words.

emergency

non-emergency

email address

website

D Work with your classmates. Look at the pictures. Circle *emergency* or *non-emergency*.

emergency   non-emergency   emergency   non-emergency   emergency   non-emergency

2 Read a city services website

A Read the city services website.

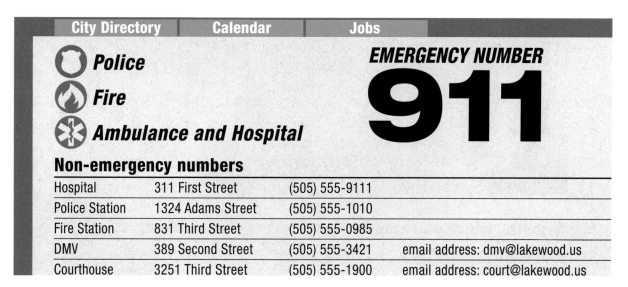

| City Directory | Calendar | Jobs |

🛡 **Police**
🔥 **Fire**
✳ **Ambulance and Hospital**

EMERGENCY NUMBER
911

Non-emergency numbers

Hospital	311 First Street	(505) 555-9111	
Police Station	1324 Adams Street	(505) 555-1010	
Fire Station	831 Third Street	(505) 555-0985	
DMV	389 Second Street	(505) 555-3421	email address: dmv@lakewood.us
Courthouse	3251 Third Street	(505) 555-1900	email address: court@lakewood.us

B Look at the website. Circle *a* or *b*.

1. For a police emergency, call _____ .
   a. 911   b. (505) 555-1010

2. The hospital is on _____ .
   a. Adams St.   b. First St.

3. The fire station is on _____ .
   a. First St.   b. Third St.

4. The non-emergency number for the hospital is _____ .
   a. (505) 555-9111 b. 911

> **READING NOTE**
> On a website, click the **tab** for new information.

Mid **City**
(677) 555-9889

 BRING IT TO LIFE

Look online. Find the phone number for your police station. Write it down.

A Work with a team. Talk about the picture. Say what you see.

B Write the words you know in the chart.

Places	Actions	Other
park	play	children

C Look up three words you don't know in a dictionary. Add them to the chart.

D **Look at the picture in A. Complete the questions and answers.**

1. **A:** _____ Ken?

   B: He's at the _____ .

   A: _____ doing?

   B: _____ .

2. **A:** _____ the children?

   B: They _____ .

   A: _____ doing?

   B: They _____ .

E **Work with a partner. Ask and answer questions about the picture in A. Use *where* and *what*.**

A: Where is Pam?

B: She's in front of the hospital.

A: What's she doing?

B: She's helping a woman.

PROBLEM SOLVING

A **Listen. Look at the picture.**

3-57

Elena's Problem

B **Work with your classmates. Help Elena.**

a. Call the police.   b. Go out.   c. Listen to music.   d. Other

12 Yes, I Can!

A LOOK AT
- Jobs
- *Can* and *can't*
- Job interview skills

LESSON 1 VOCABULARY

1 Learn the names of jobs

A Look at the pictures. What jobs do you know?

B Listen and point to the pictures.

3-58

C Listen and repeat the words.

3-58

1. gardener
2. painter
3. housekeeper

4. cashier
5. hairdresser
6. mechanic

7. truck driver
8. secretary
9. salesperson

D Say the new words with a partner.

E Work with a partner. Cover the words. Point to the picture. Say the words.

2 Talk about jobs

A Look at the picture. Complete the words.

1. h a ___ ___ d r ___ s ___ e r
2. ___ a s h ___ ___ ___
3. h ___ ___ s e k e e ___ ___ r
4. g ___ r d e ___ ___ ___
5. s ___ ___ r e t ___ ___ y

6. p ___ ___ ___ t e ___
7. ___ ___ l e s p ___ ___ s o n
8. m ___ c ___ a ___ i ___
9. t r ___ ___ k d r i ___ ___ r

B Copy the words from 2A in your notebook.

C Listen and repeat.

3-59

1. **A:** Is she a salesperson?
   B: Yes, she is.

2. **A:** Is he a housekeeper?
   B: No, he isn't. He's a painter.

D Work with a partner. Point to the pictures in 2A. Practice the conversation.

A: Is she a hairdresser?
B: Yes, she is.

A: Is he a truck driver?
B: No, he isn't. He's a painter.

E Talk to three classmates. Ask and answer the question.

A: What is your job?
B: I'm a cashier.
A: What is your job?
B: I don't have a job. I'm a student.

▸▸ TEST YOURSELF

Close your book. Write five jobs. Check your spelling.

AT WORK

1 Learn about job skills

A Look at the pictures. What jobs do you see?

🔊 **B** **Listen and repeat the words.**
3-60

1. cut hair
2. fix cars
3. drive a truck
4. paint houses

5. clean
6. sell clothes
7. take care of plants
8. use a computer

C **Look at the pictures in 1A. Complete the sentences. Use the words in the box.**

takes care of	sells	drives	uses
cuts	paints	cleans	fixes

1. A hairdresser _____ hair.
2. A painter _____ .
3. A truck driver _____ a truck.
4. A gardener _____ plants.

5. A salesperson _____ clothes.
6. A secretary _____ a computer.
7. A mechanic _____ cars.
8. A janitor _____ floors.

2 Prepare to write

🔊 3-61 **A** Listen and check the skills on the job applications.

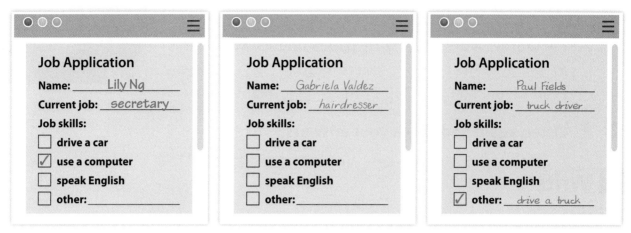

B Complete the job application. Write your current job. Check (✓) your job skills.

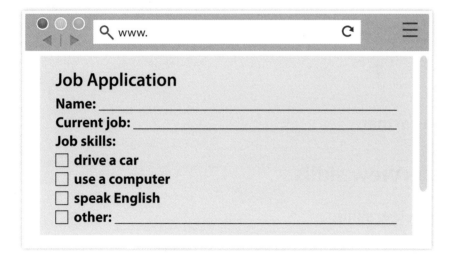

NEED HELP?

No job?
Write *None*.

🔊 3-62 **C** Listen and read Nick's paragraph.

> ### Job Skills
> I'm looking for a job. My brother is a mechanic. He fixes cars. My friend is a truck driver. She drives a truck. I can't fix cars. I can't drive a truck. But I can use a computer!

WRITER'S NOTE
Titles have capital letters.
Job **S**kills

🔊 3-63 **D** Listen to Nora's story. What can she do?

E Complete the sentences with the words in the box.

paint	types	painter
take care of	secretary	letters

My brother is a _____ . He paints houses. My sister is
a _____ . She _____ letters. I can't _____ houses.
I can't type _____ . But I can _____ plants!

Nora

F Listen again and check your answers.
3-63

3 Write

A Write a title. Think about your friends and family. Complete the paragraph.

_____

My _____ is a _____ . He can _____ . My _____ is a
_____ . She can _____ . I can't _____ . I can't _____ .
But I can _____ !

B Read your story to a partner.

AT WORK Job interview skills

A Listen. Read the interview skills.
3-64

dress appropriately   be on time   shake hands

B Work with your class. You have a job interview at 11 a.m. Discuss the questions.

What do you wear?   What time do you go?   When do you shake hands?

▶▶**TEST YOURSELF**

Copy the sentences. Choose two pictures on page 158 and complete the sentences.

He's a _____ . He can _____ . She's a _____ . She can _____ .

1 Learn about *can* and *can't*

A Listen and read the sentences.

3-65

1
He can type.

2
She can fix computers.

3
He can't cook.

4
She can't drive.

B Read the chart. Study the form.

Can and *can't*		
I You He She It We They	can can't	cut hair. use a computer. use a cash register.

C Work with a partner. Use the chart to make sentences.

D Look at the pictures. Complete the sentences. Use *can* or *can't*.

1. He _____ cut hair.

3. He _____ fix bicycles.

2. She _____ cut hair.

4. She _____ drive.

E Work with a partner. Talk about the pictures on this page.
Say: *I can* _____ or *I can't* _____ .

2 Practice: *yes/no* questions with *can* and *can't*

A Look at the pictures. Read the sentences.

A: Can you write in English?

B: Yes, I can.

A: Can you use a computer?

B: No, I can't.

B Study the form.

Can and *can't*		
Yes/no questions		
Can	you he she they	use a computer?

Can and *can't*		
Short answers		
Yes,	I he she they	can.
No,	I he she they	can't.

C Complete the questions and answers. Use *can* or *can't*.

1. **A:** _____ use a computer?

   B: Yes, she can.

2. **A:** _____ write in English?

   B: No, he can't.

3. **A:** _____ fix computers?

   B: Yes, they can.

4. **A:** Can you sell clothes?

   B: No, I _____ .

5. **A:** Can he drive a truck?

   B: Yes, he _____ .

6. **A:** Can she paint houses?

   B: No, she _____ .

D Work with a partner. Ask and answer questions about the pictures on page 163.

A: Can you cut hair?

B: Yes, I can.

A: Can you drive?

B: No, I can't.

3 Use *can* to talk about a schedule

A Look at the schedules. Listen to the conversations.

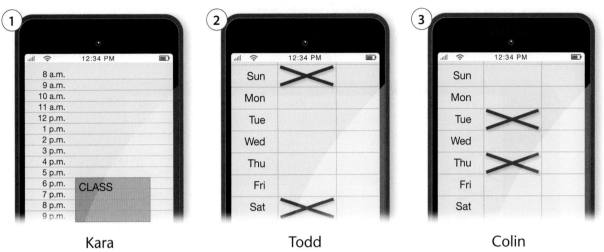

Kara   Todd   Colin

B Write answers to the questions. Then listen and check your answers.

1. **A:** Can Kara work in the morning?

 B: _____ .

 A: Can she work in the evening?

 B: _____ .

2. **A:** Can Todd work on Mondays?

 B: _____ .

 A: Can Colin work on Thursdays?

 B: _____ .

C Work with a partner. Ask and answer questions about the schedules. Use the times in the box.

at night	from 1 to 9 pm	on Tuesdays	on Fridays
on weekends	in the afternoon	on Wednesdays	from 9am to 5pm

A: Can Kara work from 1 to 9 pm?

B: Yes, she can.

A: Can Todd work on weekends?

B: No, he can't.

▸▸TEST YOURSELF

Talk to three classmates. Ask and answer questions about schedules.

Can you work on Saturdays?   *Can you work in the evening?*

1 Listen for schedule information

A Look at the schedule. When is her English class? When is her computer class?

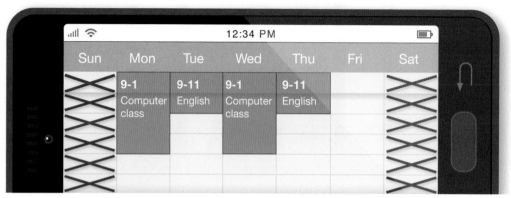

B Listen to the conversation. Circle *a* or *b*.
3-67

1. What days can she work?

   a. Monday to Friday

   b. Monday and Friday

2. What hours can she work on Monday?

   a. 8 am – 3 pm

   b. 3 pm – 10 pm

3. When can she work on Tuesday?

   a. in the morning

   b. in the afternoon

4. When can she start?

   a. Next Monday.

   b. Next Tuesday.

C Listen again. Check your answers.
3-67

2 Practice your pronunciation

A Listen for *can* and *can't*.
3-68

can	can't
I can drive.	I can't drive.
I can work.	I can't work.

B Listen and check (✓) *can* and *can't*.
3-69

	1.	2.	3.	4.	5.	6.
can	✓					
can't						

C Listen again and repeat.
3-69

3 Make conversation: answer job interview questions

A Look at the pictures. Read the conversation.

B Listen and read.

3-70

Patrick: Can you use a computer?

Silvia: Yes, I can.

Patrick: Great! What days can you work?

Silvia: I can work Monday to Saturday.

C Listen again and repeat.

3-70

D Work with a partner. Make a new conversation. Use your own ideas.

A: Can you _____ ?

B: Yes, I can.

A: What days can you work?

B: I can work _____ .

NEED HELP?

S	M	T	W	Th	F	S
	✔	✔	✔			

Monday to Wednesday

S	M	T	W	Th	F	S
	✔		✔			

Monday and Wednesday

▶▶ TEST YOURSELF

Work with a partner. Student A, look at the conversation in 3D.
Student B, close your book. Practice the conversation. Then switch roles.

1 Get ready to read

A Look at the pictures. Listen.

3-71

1 classroom aide

A classroom aide helps students.

2 babysitter

A babysitter takes care of children.

3 dental assistant

A dental assistant helps a dentist.

4 construction worker

A construction worker builds houses.

B Match.

____ 1. He builds houses.

____ 2. She takes care of children.

____ 3. He helps students.

____ 4. She helps a dentist.

a. babysitter

b. dental assistant

c. classroom aide

d. construction worker

C Look at the pictures. Read the words.

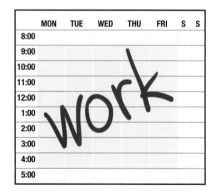

FT = full time = 40 hours per week

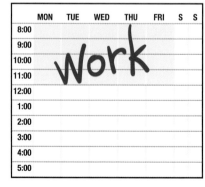

PT = part time

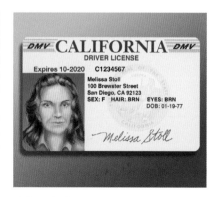

driver's license

D Circle *yes* or *no*. Use your own information.

1. Can you work full time?   yes   no
2. Can you work part time?   yes   no
3. Do you have a driver's license? yes   no

READING NOTE
The topics on a website are in a **menu**.

HIRE   JOB SEEKERS   EMPLOYERS

2 Read job ads

Look at the job ads. Check (✓) the correct ads.

FIND JOBS   **JOB SEEKERS   EMPLOYERS** ≡

(1) Dental Assistant
Dr. Kopak and Dr. Serna
FT
Good computer skills
Weekends and Evenings

(2) Babysitter
Melrose Adult School
PT
Nights/Weekends
Driver's License
Take care of children, ages 2–5

(3) Construction Worker
ACME Construction
PT
Mon., Wed., Fri. Mornings
June–September

(4) Classroom Aide
Hawaiian Gardens School
PT
Mornings, Mon. – Fri.
Help students with reading, writing, and computers.
Speak Spanish and English.

	Ad 1	Ad 2	Ad 3	Ad 4
1. work on Saturdays	☐	☐	☐	☐
2. work in the summer	☐	☐	☐	☐
3. use a computer	☐	☐	☐	☐
4. work full time	☐	☐	☐	☐
5. have a driver's license	☐	☐	☐	☐
6. work in the evening	☐	☐	☐	☐

 BRING IT TO LIFE

Look online. Find a job ad. Copy three words you know.

12:34 PM
JOBS!

A Work with a team. Talk about the pictures. Say what you see.

Lin

Kelly

Boris
你好

Al

May

Lila

B Write the words you know in the chart.

Job	Job skill	Other
cashier	use a cash register	store

C Look up three words you don't know in a dictionary. Add them to the chart.

D Talk to three classmates. Ask and answer the questions. Write your classmates' answers in your notebook.

A: What are your job skills?

B: I can take care of children. I can cook Chinese food.

Name	Job skills
Min	take care of children, cook Chinese food

E Work with your class. What skills do the students have? Put the skills in a class chart.

| We can... | | | | |
speak	cook	use	fix	other
English	Chinese food	a computer	a computer	
Arabic	Mexican food	a cash register	a lamp	

PROBLEM SOLVING

A Listen. Look at the pictures.

3-72

Adriana's Problem

B Work with your classmates. Help Adriana.

a. Say, "I can't work Saturday. It's my friend's wedding."

b. Call in sick.

c. Go to work. Don't go to the wedding.

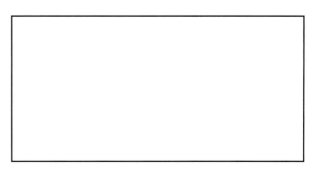

d. Other: _____

Simple present with *be*

Statements		
I	am	
You	are	a student.
He She	is	
It	is	a book.
We You They	are	students.

Negative statements		
I	am not	
You	are not	a student.
He She	is not	
It	is not	a book.
We You They	are not	students.

Contractions	
I am = I'm	I am not = I'm not
you are = you're	you are not = you're not
he is = he's	he is not = he's not
she is = she's	she is not = she's not
it is = it's	it is not = it's not
we are = we're	we are not = we're not
they are = they're	they are not = they're not

Yes/no questions		
Am	I	
Are	you	
Is	he she it	at school?
Are	we you they	

Answers					
Yes,	I	am.	No,	I	am not.
	you	are.		you	're not.
	he she it	is.		he she it	's not.
	we you they	are.		we you they	're not.

Information questions		
Where	am	I?
How	are	you?
How Where Who	is	he? she?
How long How much What What time When Where Who	is	it?
Where	are	we? you? they?

Present continuous

Statements

I	am	
You	are	
He She It	is	sleeping.
We You They	are	

Negative statements

I	am not	
You	are not	
He She It	is not	sleeping.
We You They	are not	

Yes/no questions

Am	I	
Are	you	
Is	he she it	sleeping?
Are	we you they	

Answers

Yes,	I	am.	No,	I	am not.
	you	are.		you	're not.
	he she it	is.		he she it	's not.
	we you they	are.		we you they	're not.

Information questions

What	am	I	
	are	you	
	is	he she it	doing?
	are	we you they	

The simple present

Statements

I You	like	
He She It	likes	rice.
We You They	like	

Negative statements

I You	don't		
He She It	doesn't	like	rice.
We You They	don't		

Contractions

do not = don't
does not = doesn't

Yes/no questions

Do	I you		
Does	he she it	like	rice?
Do	we you they		

Answers

Yes,	I you	do.	No,	I you	don't.
	he she it	does.		he she it	doesn't.
	we you they	do.		we you they	don't.

Can

Statements

I You He She It We You They	can	work.

Negative statements

I You He She It We You They	can't	work.

Contractions

cannot = can't

Yes/no questions

Can	I you he she it we you they	work?

Answers

Yes,	I you he she it we you they	can.	No,	I you he she it we you they	can't.

This, that, these, and those

Singular statements		Notes
This That	shirt is $35.	Use *this* and *these* when the people or things are near.

Plural statements		Notes
These Those	pants are $14.	Use *that* and *those* when the people or things are far.

A and an

Articles	
a	pencil binder
an	eraser open book

Nouns

To make plural nouns	Examples	
For most nouns, add -s.	student—students	orange—oranges
If nouns end in -s, -sh, -ch, -x, add -es.	bus—buses	box—boxes
If nouns end in consonant + y, change -y to -ies.	family—families	country—countries
If nouns end in vowel + y, keep -y.	boy—boys	day—days
Some plural nouns do not end in -s, -es, or -ies. They are irregular plurals.	child—children man—men	person—people woman—women

Subject pronouns

Subject pronouns
I
you
he
she
it
we
you
they

Possessive adjectives

Possessive adjectives
my
your
his
her
its
our
your
their

Possessives

Nouns		Notes
Gloria's Mr. and Mrs. Smith's	home is big.	For two or more nouns together, add -'s after the last noun.

Prepositions

Times and dates		Notes
The party is	on Tuesday. on Thursday.	Use *on* for days and dates. Use *at* for times.
	at 6:00. at 7:00.	

Locations			
The school is	is	on	Pine Street.
		next to	the bus station.
		between	the post office and the park.
		on the corner.	
The sofa	is	in	the living room.
		below	the window.
The window		above	the sofa.

Frequency expressions

Take two tablets	every twice a three times a	day.	
	every four hours. every six hours.		

OXFORD
UNIVERSITY PRESS

198 Madison Avenue
New York, NY 10016 USA

Great Clarendon Street, Oxford, OX2 6DP, United Kingdom

Oxford University Press is a department of the University of Oxford.
It furthers the University's objective of excellence in research, scholarship,
and education by publishing worldwide. Oxford is a registered trade
mark of Oxford University Press in the UK and in certain other countries

ISBN: 9 78 0 19 449375 8 Student Book (Pack)

ISBN: 9 78 0 19 449300 0 Student Book (Pack Component)

ISBN: 9 78 0 19 440479 2 OEVT App

Printed in China

This book is printed on paper from certified and well-managed sources

ACKNOWLEDGMENTS

Back cover photograph: Oxford University Press building/David Fisher

Illustrations by: Cover, Jeff Mangiat / Mendola Artist Representatives. 5W Infographics,
p. 20, p. 21, p. 22, p. 43, p. 57 (bottom), p. 58, p. 71 (top), p. 80, p. 81, p. 85 (bottom),
p. 99 (bottom), p. 106, p. 110, p. 112, p. 127, p. 141, p. 155 (bottom), p. 165, p. 166,
p. 169 (bottom); Shawn Banner, p. 19, p. 93, p. 108, p. 119 (bottom), p. 154 (C.),
p. 155 (top), p. 163; John Batten, p. 35, p. 77, p. 108 (bottom), p. 122; Barbara Bastian,
p. 46; Kathy Baxendale, p. 32, p. 37, p. 112 (bottom), p. 117, p.130; Arlene Boehm,
p. 2, p. 47, p. 113 (top), p. 168; Kevin Brown, p. 11, p. 38, p. 39, p. 98 (top), p. 154 (A.
and B.), p. 142; Gary Bullock, p. 33, p. 61; Richard Carbajal, p. 21 (bottom), p. 52,
p. 64 (50% off); Laurie A. Conley, p. 25 (bottom), p. 159; Phil Constantinesco, p. 147;
Mona Daly, p. 66; Bill Dickson, p. 23, p. 62, p. 94, p. 126 (A.), p. 152, p. 160; Jody
Emery, p. 42, p. 69 (bottom), p. 111 (bottom); Mike Gardner, p. 9, p. 11, p. 42, p. 48,
p. 69, p. 70, p. 98, p. 113, p. 118, p. 119, p. 121, p. 130, p. 139, p. 142, p. 152, p. 157;
John Goodwin, p. 34, p. 45, p. 67, p. 90, p. 92, p. 137; Glenn Gustafson, p. 162;
Colin Hayes, p. 43 (Carlos), p. 113 (bottom); Kevin Hopgood, p. 13, p. 31, p. 69 (top),
p. 91, p. 101, p. 157, p. 167; Janos Jantner, p. 16, p. 86, p. 151; Ken Joudrey/Munro
Campagna, p. 140 (top); John Kurtz, p. 17, p. 51, p. 52, p. 65 (top), p. 120 (right);
Jeffrey Lindberg,p. 123, p. 170; Deb Lofaso, p. 28, p. 29, p. 50 (left), p. 53, p. 57 (top),
p. 58, p. 85 (top), p. 105, p. 120 (left), p. 138, p. 169 (middle); Daniel Long, p. 99 (top),
p. 132, p. 133, p. 136, p. 145; Jeff Mangiat/Mendola Art, p. 72, p. 100; Jay Mazhar,
p. 3, p. 97, p. 118, p. 125, p. 139 (top); Karen Minot, p. 155 (middle); Jay Montgomery,
p. 144; Marc Mones, p. 24, p. 25, p. 34, p. 84, p. 119 (top); Terry Paczko, p. 60, p. 68,
p. 88, p. 116; Pamorama.com, p. 8, p. 9, p. 10, p. 40, p. 135 (top), p. 140 (bottom); Geo
Parkin, p. 18, p. 19, p. 41, p. 44, p. 59, p. 63, p. 87, p. 114, p. 129, p. 143, p. 150, p. 153,
p. 156; Roger Penwill, p. 45, p. 73, p. 115, p. 171; Pixelation Digital Imagery, p. 54,
p. 71 (bottom), p. 99 (right), p. 124; Karen Pritchett, p. 74, p. 102, p. 103 (top); Marthe
Roberts, p. 49 (bottom), p. 96, p. 125 (C.); Jon Rogers/AA Reps, p. 109; Aaron Sacco, p. xiii,
p. 50 (right), p. 78, p. 83, p. 95; Martin Sanders, p. 146; Don Stewart, p. 75; Jeff Wack/
Mendola Art, p. 72, p. 128; William Waitzman, p. 14, p. 15, p. 48, p. 70 (top), p. 104,
p. 126 (B.); Wendy Wassink, p. 109; Simon Williams/Illustration Ltd., p. 5, p. 30, p. 65
(bottom), p. 89, p. 131, p. 135 (bottom), p. 158; Ron Zalme, p. 27 (top), p. 55, p. 79,
p. 83, p. 98 (bottom), p. 103 (bottom), p. 111 (top), p. 121.

*The publishers would like to thank the following for their kind permission to reproduce
photographs*: Click Bestsellers / Shutterstock.com, Cover; pixelheadphoto
digitalskillet/Shutterstock.com, p. 2 (african-american woman); Marcin Sylwia
Ciesielski/Shutterstock.com, p. 2 (blonde woman); Blend Images/Alamy Stock Photo,
p. 2 (eldery woman); Sergey Mironov/Alamy Stock Photo, p. 2 (person writing);
ARENA Creative/Shutterstock.com, p. 2 (man reading); robertmandel/Getty Images,
p. 2 (teacher); cate_89/Shutterstock.com, p. 2 (couple); Hero Images Inc./Alamy
Stock Photo, p. 2 (students); Daniel M Ernst/Shutterstock.com, p. 5 (student); Syda
Productions/Shutterstock.com, p. 5 (teacher); enc/Shutterstock.com, p. 5 (book);
Redko Evgeniya/Shutterstock.com, p. 5 (pen); Ruslan Ivantsov/Shutterstock.com,
p. 5 (pencil); Retrovizor/Getty Images, p. 5 (paper); Hero Images Inc./Alamy Stock
Photo, p. 7 (students); Image Source/Alamy Stock Photo, p. 9 (man); Burlingham/
Shutterstock.com, p. 9 (woman); Glow Asia RF/Alamy Stock Photo, p. 9 (two women);
gutsulyak/Shutterstock.com, p. 9 (books); Andrew Unangst/Alamy Stock Photo,
p. 9 (pencil & paper); MBI/Alamy Stock Photo, p. 9 (father & son); ImageDB/Alamy
Stock Photo, p. 12 (name tag); Pylyp Fomin/Alamy Stock Vector, p. 12 (name tag);
rangizzz/Shutterstock.com, p. 12 (name tag); Mega Pixel/Shutterstock.com, p. 12
(name tag); kyoshino/Getty Images, p. 14 (binder); NATTHAWUT PUNYOSAENG/
Alamy Stock Photo, p. 14 (notebook); endeavor/Shutterstock.com, p. 14 (eraser);
kyoshino/Getty Images, p. 15 (binder); NATTHAWUT PUNYOSAENG/Alamy Stock
Photo, p. 15 (notebook); endeavor/Shutterstock.com, p. 15 (eraser); Yulia Glam/
Shutterstock.com, p. 19 (happy face); Yulia Glam/Shutterstock.com, p. 19 (sad face);
JARED LAZARUS/KRT/Newscom, p. 21 (Haitian woman); Juanmonino/Getty Images,
p. 22 (middle eastern woman); Jose Luis Pelaez Inc/Getty Images, p. 23 (happy man);
Asiaselects/Getty Images, p. 23 (sick woman); Phoenixns/Shutterstock.com, p. 23
(tired students); flower travelin' man/Shutterstock.com, p. 27 (emoticons); Leyasw/
Shutterstock.com, p. 30 (map); Tom Antos/Shutterstock.com, p. 36 (laundromat);
Image Source/Alamy Stock Photo, p. 37 (student); Erik Swanson/Alamy Stock Photo,
p. 37 (man); OzonE_AnnA/Shutterstock.com, p. 37 (clock); DAHL PHOTO/Alamy Stock
Photo, p. 37 (mother & daughter); Dean Drobot/Shutterstock.com, p. 37 (students in
library); Blend Images/Alamy Stock Photo, p. 37 (doctor); Monkey Business Images/
Shutterstock.com, p. 39 (supermarket); Monkey Business Images/Shutterstock.com,
p. 39 (doctor's office); Images-USA/Alamy Stock Photo, p. 42 (bus); Art Konovalov/
Shutterstock.com, p. 42 (car); best images/Shutterstock.com, p. 42 (airplane);
Matthew Clarke/Alamy Stock Photo, p. 42 (train); Radius Images/Alamy Stock
Photo, p. 50 (man); Blend Images/Alamy Stock Photo, p. 53 (doctor); DragonImages/
Getty Images, p. 53 (dentist); Blend Images/Alamy Stock Photo, p. 53 (hairdresser);
Uncle Leo/Shutterstock.com, p. 54 (MLK); Vereshchagin Dmitry/Shutterstock.
com, p. 56 (garage); Monkey Business Images/Shutterstock.com, p. 56 (restaurant);
Corepics VOF/Shutterstock.com, p. 56 (hotel); Ronnie Kaufman/Getty Images,
p. 64 (man); Banprik/Shutterstock.com, p. 67 (towel); timquo/Shutterstock.com,
p. 67 (towels); Aboutnuy Love/Shutterstock.com, p. 67 (razor); Natalia Rezanova/
Shutterstock.com, p. 67 (razors); You Touch Pix of EuToch/Shutterstock.com, p. 67
(comb); design56/Shutterstock.com, p. 67 (combs); Floortje/Getty Images, p. 67
(brush); Africa Studio/Shutterstock.com, p. 67 (brushes); nmphoto/Shutterstock.
com, p. 75 (man); Panther Media GmbH/Alamy Stock Photo, p. 75 (woman); Digital
Vision./Getty Images, p. 76 (wedding); Westend61 GmbH/Alamy Stock Photo, p. 76
(woman); Milosz_G/Shutterstock.com, p. 76 (divorce); Michael Prince/Getty Images,
p. 76 (man); James Leynse/Getty Images, p. 76 (man); Utah-based Photographer
Ryan Houston/Getty Images, p. 76 (woman); AJR_photo/Shutterstock.com, p. 76
(woman); YAY Media AS/Alamy Stock Photo, p. 76 (woman); iofoto/Shutterstock.
com, p. 76 (woman); Charles Wollertz/Alamy Stock Photo, p. 80 (California); Tara
Moore/Getty Images, p. 80 (New York); bikeriderlondon/Shutterstock.com, p. 80
(Texas); Spotmatik/Alamy Stock Photo, p. 80 (Florida); MIXA/Alamy Stock Photo,
p. 84 (kindergarten children); Monkey Business Images/Shutterstock.com, p. 84
(elementary children); KidStock/Getty Images, p. 84 (middle school children);
David Schaffer/Getty Images, p. 84 (high school children); Troscha/Shutterstock.
com, p. 90 (cheese); gillmar/Shutterstock.com, p. 90 (eggs); Elisabeth Burrell/Alamy
Stock Photo, p. 90 (milk); StockPhotosArt/Shutterstock.com, p. 90 (bread); Valentina
Razumova/Shutterstock.com, p. 90 (chicken); Diana Taliun/Shutterstock.com, p. 90
(pork); Pamela D. Maxwell/Shutterstock.com, p. 90 (beef); Edward Westmacott/
Shutterstock.com, p. 90 (lamb); yukibockle/Shutterstock.com, p. 90 (rice); Jade/
Getty Images, p. 92 (soup); tiverylucky/Shutterstock.com, p. 93 (boy & chicken);
Hemant Mehta/Getty Images, p. 93 (boy & milk); ESB Professional/Shutterstock.com,
p. 93 (boy & vegetables); PeopleImages/Getty Images, p. 93 (children & vegetables);
Foodstock/Alamy Stock Photo, p. 95 (cheese); Tastyart Ltd Rob White/Getty
Images, p. 95 (pork chops); amenic181/Shutterstock.com, p. 95 (chicken); Robyn
Mackenzie/Shutterstock.com, p. 95 (steak); Rudchenko Liliia/Shutterstock.com, p. 95
(eggs); mangostock/Shutterstock.com, p. 107 (man with backache); YAKOBCHUK
VIACHESLAV/Shutterstock.com, p. 107 (woman with toothache); Halfpoint/
Shutterstock.com, p. 107 (sick couple); Pablo Calvog/Shutterstock.com, p. 107
(woman with backache); Aleksandra Suzi/Shutterstock.com, p. 107 (sick couple);
g-stockstudio/Getty Images, p. 107 (man with toothache); CHAjAMP/Shutterstock.
com, p. 107 (woman with stomachache); Blend Images/Alamy Stock Photo, p. 107
(woman with headache); AtnoYdur/Getty Images, p. 107 (sick man); jarih/Getty
Images, p. 120 (man feeding birds); MBI/Alamy Stock Photo, p. 134 (woman in park);
Phonlamai Photo/Shutterstock.com, p. 134 (smoke alarm); HARNZING/Shutterstock.
com, p. 134 (fire extinguisher); zhu difeng/Shutterstock.com, p. 134 (caution sign);
Tetra Images/Getty Images, p. 148 (man); Helen King/Getty Images, p. 148 (man
making copies); Zero Creatives/Getty Images, p. 148 (janitor); Blend Images/Alamy
Stock Photo, p. 148 (clerk & customer); Rob Wilkinson/Alamy Stock Photo, p. 149
(woman); Claire Lucia/Shutterstock.com, p. 149 (man drinking water); g-stockstudio/
Shutterstock.com, p. 149 (businessmen talking); msderrick/Getty Images, p. 150
(man eating); Sjale/Shutterstock.com, p. 150 (couple walking); piyapong tulachom/
Shutterstock.com, p. 150 (woman writing); Image Werks Co.,Ltd./Alamy Stock
Photo, p. 151 (woman working); Andrey_Popov/Shutterstock.com, p. 151 (students);
Srdjan Fot/Shutterstock.com, p. 162 (woman gardening); MIKA Images/Alamy Stock
Photo, p. 163 (typing); Phovoir/Shutterstock.com, p. 163 (fixing computer); Mike
Kemp/Getty Images, p. 163 (burned cookies); Marcel Jancovic/Shutterstock.com,
p. 163 (baby driving car); pan_kung/Shutterstock.com, p. 164 (woman interviewing);
Monkey Business Images/Shutterstock.com, p. 164 (man interviewing); michaeljung/
Shutterstock.com, p. 168 (aide & student); Cultura Creative (RF)/Alamy Stock
Photo, p. 168 (babysitter & child); Jochen Tack/Alamy Stock Photo, p. 168 (dentist &
assistant); goodluz/Shutterstock.com, p. 168 (construction worker).